This Country Girl

BY DONNA C. MERRIAM

To Carrie

Donna C. Merriam

9-17-05

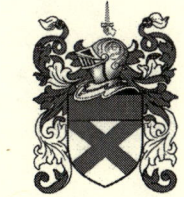

TATE PUBLISHING, LLC

"This Country Girl" by Donna C. Merriam

Copyright © 2005 by Donna C. Merriam. All rights reserved.

Published in the United States of America
by Tate Publishing, LLC
127 East Trade Center Terrace
Mustang, OK 73064
(888) 361–9473

Book design copyright © 2005 by Tate Publishing, LLC. All rights reserved.

No part of this publication may be reproduced, stored in a retrieval system or transmitted in any way by any means, electronic, mechanical, photocopy, recording or otherwise without the prior permission of the author except as provided by USA copyright law.

This book is designed to provide accurate and authoritative information with regard to the subject matter covered. This information is given with the understanding that neither the author nor Tate Publishing, LLC is engaged in rendering legal or professional advice. Since the details of your situation are fact dependent, you should additionally seek the services of a competent professional.

ISBN: 1–5988603–5-6

In Memory Of My Parents

John F. Nielsen

&

Esther (Betty) Nielsen

Acknowledgments

I would like to acknowledge the assistance of June and Philip Bays for the preliminary editing of this book.

Table Of Contents

CHAPTER ONE—CHILDHOOD

The Farm	13
The Ponies	16
The Lord's Prayer	19
Robert's Homecoming	20
The Despised Outhouse	21
Christmas and Candy	22
Snow, Snow, Snow	25
Chickens—Big and Little	27
The Wonderful Pig Lot	29
Music, Music, Music	30
Church and Pennies	34
Making Money	36
Grocery Shopping and Eating	43
Old Cars	46
The Barn and Haying Season	48
School and Education	51
Clothes and Hair	54
Fun Times	55
Doctors and Being Sick	60
The House	62
No-No-None	64
Pets of all Kinds	67
Leaving the Farm	74

CHAPTER TWO—NURSES' TRAINING
Study and Work 77

CHAPTER THREE—THE ARMY NURSE CORPS
Basic Training—Overview 91
The Green Record Book 96
Heidelberg, Germany 187
Leonard 188
Travel in Europe 190
To the States 195

CHAPTER FOUR—CIVILIAN LIFE
Ohio 197
Jail Nurse—California 199
Jeep Fun 215
Start Life Again 217
Davenport, Iowa 218
Jim 218
Start Life all Over—Again 223
California Calling 225
A Better Life—Maybe 226
Tom 227
Columbus, Ohio and DOD 232
Daddy 234
Life Goes On 235
Heart Trouble Coming 237
My Mother 239
Heart Trouble—Again 243
Thinking About Retirement 244
Retirement 245

My Mother—Again	250
Business	257
Places I Have Lived	259
Animals and Pets in Adulthood	261
Family Ties	268
Endings	273

Introduction

This book is a factual and true story.
This book is written by a baby boomer for baby boomers and all ages.
It tells of a country childhood in America, during and after WWII.
It tells of the triumphs and travails of becoming a registered nurse.
It provides a daily record of Army Nurse Corps Basic Training of 40 years ago.
It remembers lost loves.
It tells of the trials of marriage.
It tells of 40 years of living and working after the completion of school.
It emphasizes family life, love, and support.
It relates a lifelong love affair with various animals and birds.
It shows the joy of knowing that you have eternal life.

Chapter One - Childhood

THE FARM

My childhood has many, many fond memories. There were four of us kids. I had a brother, John, four years older, a sister, June, two years older and a brother, Robert, four years younger than myself. Mother and Daddy were selfless and raised a fine family. Without them, we would not have had the many fine memories that we each cherish.

We lived on a 160-acre farm in the middle of the fields. We had a half mile gravel lane, and it was about a half mile in any other direction from our house to the road or to our neighbors. We had neighbors on all four sides of our farm, but we seldom saw them.

The four of us learned to play amongst ourselves. We developed a closeness that remains to this day.

I loved the farm. It had a large barnyard area, a delightful pig lot, a pony lot, a cow pasture, a spring pasture, and a chicken yard. It also had many fields in which we planted corn, soy beans, hay, and oats.

There were a number of buildings on the property. The house was a two-story dwelling with a basement, a long porch on one side, and a small porch on the front. The chicken house was to the left of the front porch as you came out of the house. The chicken yard was next to the house yard, and there was a path leading from the house to the outhouse, which set next to the chicken house. To the right of the house, across the lawn and a machinery driveway, was the brooder house. This had its own small yard. To the right of the barnyard was a garage with a dirt floor and a larger machine shop next to it. Further down on the right was a huge maple tree that had all kinds of junk and machinery laying beneath it—always an interesting place to play and to look for new additions.

Even further down on the right was a corncrib, an oblong, slotted affair with a corn elevator going up to the roof. This crib was used for whole ear storage. There was also a round, unused bin located to the east of the corncrib.

At the opposite end of the barnyard from the house and north of the corncrib was the barn. As a child it looked huge, but I noticed when I went back later in life that it really was a rather small structure.

To the left of the barn was the pony lot. It consisted of two large areas with a hedge in between. It had rolling hills. This sounds huge, described with the term "rolling hills." But as a child, it seemed that way. The first section held the pump that provided us with our drinking water. Behind the barn was the pig lot that went to the south along the fields for a long way. Behind the machine shop and the garage area was a cow pasture which led down to the spring pasture.

That was the layout of the farm. I will be referring to other parts in subsequent sections. A diagram is provided below.

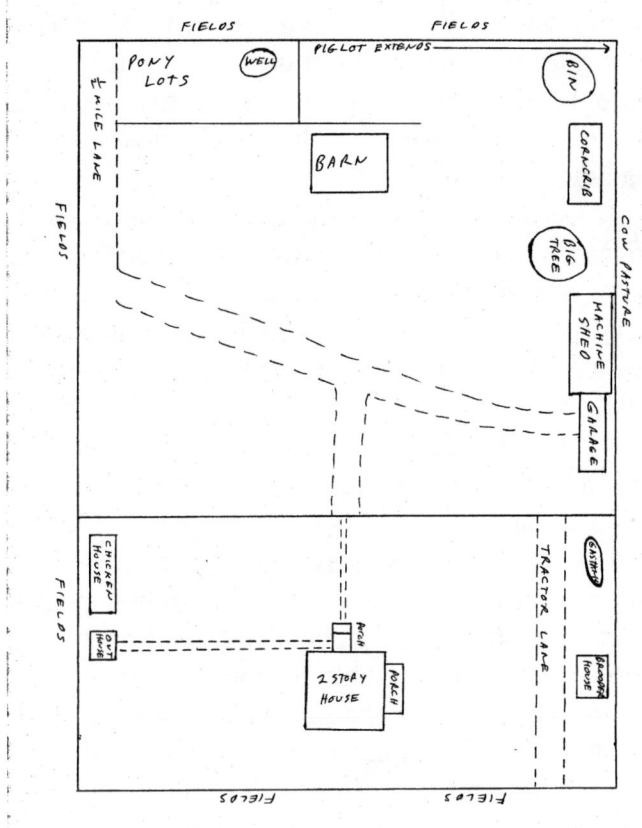

THE PONIES

We had two ponies. The female was Sandy, and she gave birth to a male colt we named Dusky. Sandy was brown while Dusky was a very dark brown. One of my earliest memories was the day Dusky was born. I was about four, and mother carried me down to the barn to see the new colt as the ground was very muddy.

As the colt grew, so did I. John was old enough to teach Dusky to be ridden. One of my very favorite pictures is of me sitting on the back of Dusky at a very young age. Dusky was strong and spirited. John and I rode the most. June and Robert did not care for riding as much.

We learned to ride bareback as we had only one old saddle, and it only fit Sandy. Sandy later became crippled, and we could not ride her much. We had been to church one Sunday and came home to find the gate of the pony lot wide open, and both ponies were loose. They had gone behind the barn by the corncrib. As I understand the story, Sandy ate corn and then drank water and became "foundered." As a result, her hooves would grow out real long and curl upward. This made it difficult and probably painful for her to walk. Daddy would have to saw them off with a saw every so often and trim them to shape with a file. Rather a long, hard job. That is why we usually rode Dusky and did it bareback.

I used to ride up in the fields when the cattle were allowed out in the corn fields after husking. I would ride on Dusky to bring the cattle back to the barn cow yard. My dog, Rex, would go with me and help to round up the cattle and drive them back. That is such a very fond memory. At that time of year, it was fall and crisp and cold. Sometimes we already would have snow on the ground. John used to do this too.

One of the times Robert was riding and maybe the reason he did not really enjoy it was because Dusky got tangled up with bees and got stung. I guess Robert had a fast, hard ride that day. I used that incident to my advantage. We found out that if we took a half-round red tube of BBs and shook it by Dusky's ear he would run. So we usually carried one with us if we wanted some speed.

Dusky was strong and sometimes hard for me to hold and control. Once I had ridden him up the lane and across the field to the fence by Wiesbrock's property. We sat and looked across, and I could feel Dusky tensing his muscles. When we turned, he went at a full gallop down the field, skidded around the gravel curve leading toward the barnyard, went around the barn, and came back of it. Then he stopped dead. That was when I fell off. I never forgot that ride.

I loved Dusky and riding, but I, too, was a little scared as I did not have the strength as a child to control him. Shetland ponies can be pretty stubborn.

We also used to tie Dusky up in the lane between the house and the brooder house. One time he ran down there because he knew he would get to rest. Well, he ran under a tree branch, and my hair, which was up in a ponytail, caught in a branch. It lifted me right off his back. That hurt.

Cousins and friends used to enjoy coming to visit and getting a pony ride. Daddy would put them on Sandy's back, using the saddle, and lead them up and down the barnyard.

Robert and I used to play together when he got old enough. I would ride Dusky, and he would run alongside up and down the hills in the pony lot and into the barnyard. We would use toy guns and cap guns and bow and arrows to play cowboys and Indians. We had old holsters to use, and we always looked very correct. Our arrows were always homemade. I would search long and hard to find the straightest and most sturdy stick I could come up with. We would cut a notch in the end to fit the string, and it worked fine.

Another major story about Dusky occurred during winter. When John, June, and I were little and it snowed hard and the lane was blocked, Daddy would put the three of us on Dusky's back. He would lead the pony up to the end of the lane and wait there with us until the school bus came. Once in awhile it did not come, and he would lead us back home. On occasion, we walked across the fields to Wiesbrocks to wait in their house. We never missed school unless school itself was cancelled, which was not very often. Girls were not allowed to wear slacks to school, but in the really cold weather, we would put them on under our skirts and then take them off when we got to school.

Sandy and Dusky loved to eat sugar cubes, carrots, apples, and bread. We enjoyed giving these to them when we had them. They had a very large, two-section, hilly pony lot. The grass was green and they had plenty of room to run. They were beautiful and I loved them.

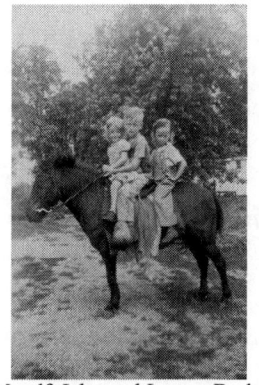
Myself, John, and June on Dusky.

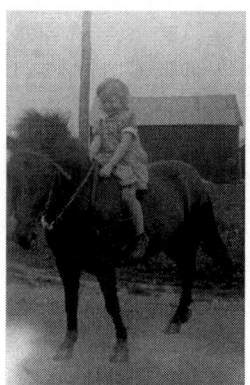
Me on Dusky.

THE LORD'S PRAYER

Another of my earlier memories concerned "The Lord's Prayer." I am not certain at what age this was, but I was pretty little. I was standing in the middle of our living room, and mother was sitting on one of the chipped, white wooden chairs from the kitchen, in front of the brown desk. I was supposed to be reciting "The Lord's Prayer" by heart, and I kept messing up. I can hear her saying that she would spank me if I did not do it right. I guess she was at her wits end. I do not know if I ever said it right that day, but I do know it now.

ROBERT'S HOMECOMING

Another early memory was when I was four. Charlene (our babysitter) and I were standing, looking out the front window of the house. It was cold out because Mother and Daddy were coming up the sidewalk and were dressed in coats. They had a bundle with them, and Charlene told me that that was my new brother, Robert.

My next memory of Robert was of Mother nursing Robert upstairs in the bedroom, and we had to wear a mask to see him. I think there was measles in the house.

The next memory I have of Robert was when he was very little and afraid to go to the outhouse at night. I would have to take him out to the front sidewalk so he could go if it was a little job.

Mother always told us the story about the gas cook stove. It had knobs that you had to push in to turn a burner on. She was always very secure that we could not do this when we were small. However, she said that I proceeded to teach Robert how to turn them on long before he needed to know.

Then I don't remember much else about Robert until he was old enough to play with me and the pony.

THE DESPISED OUTHOUSE

This is the one building on the farm that I hated so much but had to go into numerous times, day and night. It is the place that affected me negatively every day of my life and will until my dying day.

This little building was about the size of two—three telephone booths across. It had three holes. The one on the right side as you are going in was small and had a step up for the little kids to reach. Then there was a medium and a large size. For little kids the large one always carried the fear of falling in.

I always went in the door straight to the center one so I did not have to touch the walls. There was a pull string for the overhead light bulb, but it was dark, even with the light on. The place was full of cobwebs with huge spiders of all kinds. I was so scared of them, but there was not anything I could do about them. All of my life since then I have been truly terrified of any spider. Every day they are in my thoughts no matter where I go or what I do. I've learned to check an area before entering. I have a real phobia about them and cannot tolerate even talking about them or being teased about them. I find it very hard to even write this.

Because of the outhouse I have always also been a little claustrophobic. I think it is mainly due to the thought of being confined to a small space and maybe finding a spider in there with me. I could not handle that.

Several other things about the outhouse should

be mentioned. When we ran out of toilet paper we used the flimsy pages from a Sears catalog.

In the winter when it was really cold and nasty outside at night we had a chamber pot with a lid that we kept upstairs in the house. We used that and then it was emptied and rinsed out in the morning.

We also used a kerosene lantern at night to go out to the outhouse because the path between the house and the outhouse was dark. I was always afraid I would meet a cow on my way out or on the return trip. I would usually run as fast as I could and get there quickly or I would go just behind the hedge, near the house, if it was a little job.

Of all of my life experiences I can truly say that this outhouse impacted me the most on a continuing daily basis for my whole life. It was a totally negative impact.

CHRISTMAS AND CANDY

As we were growing up those two things always went together in my mind.

Mother and Daddy never had any money, but yet each year they made Christmas a special time for us. With everything else they had going on, a person must appreciate all the effort they put into the Christmas season.

We always had a cut tree even if we got it the day before Christmas. It was always a nice big tree. Daddy always used a big, white salt block to put the tree in, to hold it steady and upright. He sure knew how to make that work.

We all helped to decorate the tree with lights and balls and trimmings. We used the same decorations year after year, and we each had our favorite pieces. We put angel hair over the top of everything, and it gave the tree an unreal glow all over, which I can never forget.

Mother and Daddy could never afford much for presents but somewhere they found the money so each of us got at least one gift under the tree. One year, June and I each got a big beautiful doll. How I loved that doll and played with it. As it shows now, I played with it a lot. I believe June has the dolls now and has tried to preserve them for her granddaughter, Elizabeth. One year we got a miniature stove and cook set. Another year we got a set of tiny dishes, white with an emblem on them. I say "we" because I am not sure now who got what.

We children learned to share our belongings. Many times we only had one of an item for all four of us to use. They were probably Christmas gifts too. Some of these items were the red bike, the wooden sled, the BB gun, the scooter, and I am sure many more. We also had board games that we played with until they fell apart. One example is Monopoly. June always won. When we would argue, mother would threaten to take the game or item away. To prevent this from happening, we usually settled down and resolved our differences.

Some years Christmas came along and Mother

and Daddy had no money. I can remember one year a refund gas check came in the day before Christmas, so on Christmas Eve they took us shopping so we would have some gifts under the tree.

I believe Daddy even had a Santa suit that he wore, and it was always a big secret as to how the gifts got under the tree. We believed in Santa Clause until we started school. Each one of us helped to keep the secret from the younger child. Mother and Daddy always felt that we should know the truth before some kid at school told us. It was the same with the Easter Bunny and the Tooth Fairy.

My most favorite Christmas memory involves me being sneaky and not quite on the level. Each year mother would buy hard candy and chocolates and other pieces of candy. She mixed these all up in a big, white enamel pan with a lid. Then she put this pan in the spare room upstairs, so it would not melt. Every so often, she would get a small bowl of it to bring downstairs to enjoy. Sad to say, I used to go up and sneak pieces of candy out of the pan. I was smart enough to never take very much at a time, but I did always take chocolates. I don't know if they ever knew I did that, but I probably owe each of the other kids a lot of candy to this day.

Another candy story involves Christmas as well as other times during the year. Mother made fudge every once in awhile. We would all wait in great anticipation to lick the pan. Since we tended to fight about it, mother had three or four spoons and would scrape out equal amounts so we each got our share. We would also receive an equal number of pieces after it hardened. Boy was that ever good. She could always make a good batch. I made it myself for years, but have not made it for a long time now.

Christmas would never be complete without mentioning church. We were raised in the church and went every Sunday. At Christmastime, we seemed to always take part in the play at church in one way or another. Sometimes we even had lines to say or to sing. Mother and Daddy were always there to back us and to watch us, and they always let all of us know how proud they were of us. They were proud of us our whole lives, no matter what we did. They showed it and said it. We had true love in our family.

SNOW, SNOW, SNOW

It seemed years ago when I was little that we got a lot more snow in Illinois than they do today, or maybe my size gave me a different perspective. In any case, as a child, we had lots of snow. We had drifts that went up a side of a building. We had snow that we could build snow forts in. They were more like rooms with maybe a tunnel. We bundled up as warm as we could and went out all the time to play. We, of course, had the usual snowball fights, and we made angels in the snow.

We had one wooden sled that we all used and loved. We would take it down to the spring pasture where there were bigger hills to slide down. We always had to be careful as there was a spring at the bottom, and we were cautioned to stay out of that.

We had the half-mile lane and never did have a snow plow. I can remember many a time when Daddy would shovel out a place for the car, all of the way down the whole lane. Maybe they had to get out for an important thing such as Eastern Star. Mother and Daddy never let difficulties get the best of them. They always coped.

Once in a while, we would have a real blizzard, and school would be called off. We never had a phone. Sometimes we would hear it on the radio, and sometimes we went across the fields to the Wiesbrocks' house to find out. On those days, we would set a table by the stove in the front room and sit around it playing canasta or euchre. Sometimes the electricity would go out, and we would get a kerosene lantern out to play by or to get around the house.

Some mornings you would wake up and the whole world was covered in ice. Every wire, blade of grass, tree limb, and every other thing was covered in ice. So beautiful!

We had to wash clothes, even in the winter. We washed clothes in the basement, and took the clothes outside to hang on the lines. In the winter, they froze stiff as a board on the line. Sometimes when the weather was really bad, we hung clothes lines in the house all across the front room and hung everything inside to dry. Thinking back, I don't know how mother was able to keep up with all the laundry for six people.

Of course, we all had our chores to do even in winter. Daddy had milking and caring for the larger animals. We kids helped with the chickens and smaller animals and sometimes the bigger ones too. Daddy was a very strong, capable person and did his work and never complained.

CHICKENS—BIG AND LITTLE

Inside the brooder house there was a hood with a light underneath it to keep the baby chicks warm. We had glass jars of water turned over on the glass tray that was used to water the chicks. We had long metal trays where we put the mash in for food.

Every spring we would go to the hatchery in Lostant and get about 100 chicks. They were so cute. Most were yellow, but once in awhile, one was black. Of course, we played with them as we did our chores. After they got bigger, then we would move them over to the main chicken house on the opposite side of our house. There they had a yard where they could roam during the day. Every evening they all started going inside to roost, and then we closed the doors.

The roost was an area that took up most of the chicken house and was up off the floor. The chickens would settle on it to sleep for the night. At one end of the chicken house was row after row of boxes on the wall. We kept straw in these, and the chickens went in to nest and to lay their eggs. We collected the eggs every day. Sometimes you had to reach under the hen to get the eggs, and sometimes you got your hand pecked.

The chickens had water, mash, and cracked corn inside. Outside they pecked around on the ground. We kept all our table scraps, which we called slop, and gave that to the chickens too. Nothing went to waste with them.

Once in a while, a chicken would get out and build a nest somewhere outside, and every so often, we would have a mother hen followed by a bunch of chicks. I expect predators got some of them.

We locked the chickens up every night to protect them. I've heard the story that one night Johnny woke up to hear the chickens raising a ruckus out in the chicken house. Daddy and John took the shotgun out and found that a weasel had been locked up with the chickens. I don't know if they got the weasel or if it got away.

Mother had an egg route in Peru. We collected the eggs and took them down to the basement where we had to wash them and then pack them in cartons so she could transport them in the car. I think she charged fifty cents a dozen. She had the daily route for a long time. It was a lot of work getting them ready and taking them to town. Of course, we also ate eggs every day as part of our diet.

We had an old railroad tie on one side of the chicken yard that had two nails in one end, fairly close together. On special occasions, we would have chicken for a meal. Daddy put the chicken's head between the two nails and chopped it off with an axe.

The body flopped around on the ground for a bit. Then we had a big round tub that we held the chicken over and poured boiling water over it to soften the feathers. Then we could pull out all the feathers, making sure we also got all the pin feathers. Mother would take the chicken inside and cut at the tail end and remove all the insides. If she did it right, she did not break anything open inside the chicken such as the intestine. The lower legs were cut off. We kept certain parts of the insides for eating such as the heart, liver, and gizzard. It was quite an ordeal to dress and clean a chicken, and Mother was expert at it. Boy, we all loved dinner when we had a chicken.

We also prepared chickens for sale. I think we did this every year and made some extra money.

THE WONDERFUL PIG LOT

The pig lot extended from the fresh water well in the pony lot, across the back of the barnyard, and a long ways down alongside of the fields. One of the truly terrific features was the stream that ran continuously. It never dried up. It ran the full length of the pig lot. There was one bend in the stream that we were told to stay out of because it was like quicksand. We put several very long poles down in that area and never did reach the bottom. We imagined all kinds of things getting stuck in there and disappearing forever.

I spent as much of my childhood as I could down in the pig lot. I played and discovered all kinds of things. My dog Rex and I explored there all the time, and Rex would sometimes catch rabbits.

There were many frogs, and I put a few turtles in the stream. I also put some gold fish down in a big hole in the stream beneath a huge tree. Evidently, it did not freeze all the way to the bottom, because these fish got quite big and lasted year after year.

The pig lot was rather hilly, and there was an old dead tree sitting all by itself on one hill, not directly by the stream. This tree and area was my personal burial grounds. If I found a dead bird or cat or any other animal, I would take it there and leave it. Sometimes, I put them in a sack and tucked them in a nook of the tree. I just left them for the weather to take care of. I guess if anyone, years later, saw it, they might wonder how so many bones accumulated in one place.

The pig lot was my serenity, a place I could go alone, to think and to explore. I knew every inch of that place. There was a row of hedges between it and the fields. Each year I located every birds nest and watched them until the babies hatched.

The pig lot remains to this day the place of my fondest memories.

MUSIC, MUSIC, MUSIC

I guess my musical career could be divided into three areas—none of which I really excelled in.

The first would be playing the piano. Our grandmother, Martha (on mother's side), was a piano teacher and a very accomplished pianist herself. So naturally, all four of us kids needed to learn to play piano. Like any kids, I guess we would rather play than practice, so I never did very well, though I did learn some. We all played many years growing up.

John was the one who really excelled. He learned to play well and even won the district contest in the 8th grade while he had the mumps, but that is another story. He went on to win second place in the state contest that same year.

I can still play out a tune with one hand. It is the one thing now that I wish I had kept working on and could do well now.

At one point, I recall Grandma coming to live with us for awhile. I think it was when her house burned down due to lightning. The upshot of that was that she was there to monitor our practicing too. We played more during that time.

The next area of music was my singing. I seemed to love to sing and was always singing around the house. Mother recognized that maybe that was my talent. Each one of the four of us had a talent she helped to develop and promote. Mine was voice, June's was art, John's was piano, and Robert's was voice.

At my young age, mother took me to see Ms. Lundgren in Wenona. She gave me voice lessons through grade school and high school. She realized right away that I could not carry a tune all by myself. So when she accompanied me, she inserted notes into the piece so I would stay on tune. I was so proud of my singing and did well with her help. I sang for church, PTA, Eastern Star, and many various school programs. I sang many solos, and it gave me a sense of pride and accomplishment. It also got me up on the stage in front of audiences, and I learned how to handle that as well.

I think a few of the songs I liked best to sing were *The Lord's Prayer*, *O Holy Night*, *I'll Never Walk Alone*, *Trees*, and many many more which I don't remember. To this day, when I hear a song I used to sing, I will remember.

One of my earliest performances was on Main Street in Lostant. Lostant has a population of 500, which never changes. At least the sign never changes. During the summer months, Lostant set up a movie screen across Main Street. All the people sat on the steps running along the other side, while a movie played for the people to watch. As kids, we loved to watch these movies. One time June and I were asked to sing a duet at this street gathering, and we sang "Beautiful Dreamer."

I sang for so many school and church functions that I cannot even begin to count. I also sang for the contests in the state, but I never did win the state contest. Speaking of contests, June and I each tried out for a speaking piece at the contests. June had a piece about a poor newspaper boy and his dog Patch. It was such a heartbreaking story, and she did it so well. Mine was about a sheikh, and it was humorous. We had to memorize the stories and present them. I do not remember how far we advanced with these.

One highlight in my singing was being soloist for Mother and Daddy at their Eastern Star night when they became Grand Worthy Matron and Grand Worthy Patron for the year. I sang a repertoire of songs for them. Each one of the four kids performed in some way that night for them. It was a highlight for them especially, but also for us kids. We all were dressed up beautifully. I wore my first "formal."

One dream I had all the time I was growing up was that I would become an opera singer. I don't know where that came from because, as far as I know, I had never even seen an opera. I kept that dream well into high school, before I realized I did not have a good enough voice for that. Also, it was impractical.

My third area of music was playing in the school band. I also sang in the chorus at school and in the choir at church off and on. However, band was forever, but I was never really good at it. Lostant school had such a small band that mother rather insisted we stay in the band to help them out—forever (not sure how big a help I was). Again, I believe all four of us played an instrument, which also meant more practice. I played clarinet, John played French horn and tuba, June played clarinet, and I believe Robert played the trumpet.

Playing in the band meant performing at all the school functions and at some town functions. We had to march in formation while playing our instrument. We had tiny music holders attached to our instrument that held the music. It seemed a lot to remember to try and march and play at the same time. But we did it—forever.

The last musical instrument I know mother wanted us to learn to play was the violin. She herself played and loved to play. She performed often at places in the community. None of us kids really took to the violin and never really went very far with it.

CHURCH & PENNIES

We were definitely raised in the church. We went every Sunday, and we had a pew that was always ours. It was on the furthest side of the church from the door and in the back. That is important to know, as nine times out of ten we arrived late. All six of us came streaming across the back of the church while the congregation was already singing.

We always dressed up for church. We had our Sunday best clothes and, back then, you made an effort to dress up and look nice. Daddy had one suit and he always wore it. Mother always tried to keep our Sunday best looking good. Many Sunday mornings she would be in her slip ironing Daddy's shirt or some of our clothes.

Lostant Methodist Church is a beautiful church. It has a gorgeous, big stained glass window on either side of the church and a number of other smaller stained glass windows. It has a beautiful alter and a curved kneeling rail for Communion. Beautiful wood all throughout the church. Behind the main sanctuary area was a separate room for Sunday school for the younger kids. We always went to Sunday school too. Downstairs were several large rooms and a big kitchen. Older kids had Sunday school classes there.

The downstairs was also where Mother and Daddy held their 40th and 50th wedding anniversary parties. All four of us came back to attend these, I believe. A lot of the community and many relatives also celebrated with them. Mother and Daddy were well known, were respected, and well liked all around the area. They had both grown up and lived in the area for most of their lives.

All of us kids belonged to the MYF (Methodist Youth Fellowship) and attended various parties and functions put on by them. School and MYF were the only social outlets that we attended. Take that back. We also belonged to Grange for awhile and attended their meetings and functions, but that was in another community. We did not mix with those kids very often. I am not sure even what the Grange was all about.

Back to the church, you are probably wondering where the pennies come in. Our family was very poor growing up and never had much extra money. However, Mother and Daddy always tried to have a little change to put in the collection plate each Sunday. Daddy usually put in fifteen cents for both he and mother. Mother tied up several pennies in the corner of our hankies for each of us to put in. The boys probably kept their pennies in their pockets. They felt it was important that we be raised with the understanding of giving. I know there were some

Sundays they did not have any money, and I know Daddy always felt bad about that.

MAKING MONEY

Every kid reaches a certain point when they understand about money and the fact that you need it to buy anything. At that point, you have to be old enough to do something worthwhile to earn it. As we became old enough, we were assigned chores to do, outside chores and housework.

Let us start with some of the outside chores first. We helped out on the farm all of the time. One job, which was quite boring but helped Daddy when he was plowing, was to sit at the end of the row and clean off the mud from the plow shares. We used a cob (as in corncob) to do this task. As he progressed up the field, we also moved up the rows on the end.

Another job we helped with was inoculating beans. Daddy put the beans to be planted in a big round tub. Then he opened this box of black powder and poured it on. Then he added a little water so everything would stick on the beans. Then we would dig to the bottom of the tub with our hands over and over and rotate the beans to the top until all had some black on them. Of course, our hands, arms, and probably our clothes were black too. Then Daddy used these beans to plant the bean crop (soybeans).

I loved to help with the haying season, but will devote an entire section to that as it was such a memorable time in my life. We helped to walk the fields, both corn and beans, and pulled weeds after the crop started coming up. That was hard work.

We helped to harvest the corn in several ways. Sometimes we rode in the wagon to deflect the corn to all parts of the wagon so the wagon would hold more evenly. We did the same thing up in the corn crib. The corn (whole ear) came up on an elevator to the cupola and fell into the hole in the roof. We had a piece of plywood that we could use to deflect the corn to all areas of the corn crib. Sometimes Daddy had to stop the elevator if we got backed up. It too was hard and dirty work.

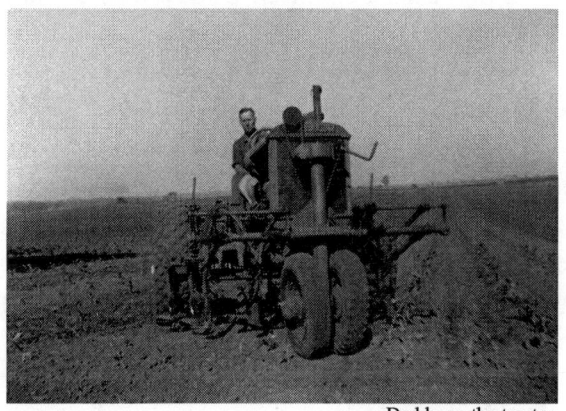

Daddy on the tractor.

Of course, our farm had animals that needed care. Daddy always did the milking every morning. We had a Guernsey milk cow. Sometimes he would squirt some in a pan for the farm cats. He always carried the bucket up to the house, and we drank the milk right from the cow. Occasionally mother would churn butter. Sometimes we helped put hay in the manger for the cows or the ponies, and sometimes we gave them oats to eat as well.

We had chickens. Chores relating to the chickens were mainly handled by us kids. As I mentioned, we collected eggs daily. We watered and fed the chickens. We made sure they were locked up for the night and let out in the morning. We cleaned out the chicken house and the nesting boxes. We helped with dressing and cleaning chickens to eat or sell.

We took care of any pets we had at the time, whether they were domestic or wild ones that we had caught.

At night, in the winter, Daddy would work on his machinery in the machine shed. Many a time I would be out there watching and holding the trouble light for him.

We had to get our own drinking water from the spring well down in the pony lot. That involved carrying this big bucket clear across the yard and barnyard, going under the fence with it, and carrying it down to the well in the pony lot while trying to stay away from the ponies. Then you lifted the bucket up on the platform and climbed up. After pumping the water with the hand pump, you then had to reverse that whole process. Sometimes in getting the bucket down from the well you tended to spill water on your clothes. By the time we got back to the house, the bucket was usually not as full as when we started. At the house, the bucket set on a shelf in the pantry with a dipper hanging on the side. The whole family just drank directly from the dipper when thirsty.

I will never forget that one time our land lady planned to dig a new well closer to the house. This man came out with a "witching stick" and walked up and down until the stick bent to water. She did have a well dug there. It was right outside the front yard, but was not drinkable. We still had to carry water from the pony lot every day, all year long, no matter what the weather was. We did use the closer well for some other uses in the house and on the farm.

We helped mother with the house work, laundry, ironing, and some cooking. One job she always gave us, which I hated, was cleaning the baseboards. Our baseboards were tall and had all kinds of ridges and crevices and designs to clean. I pulled a bucket of water and a cloth and scooted all around wiping down the baseboards. It was a big house and a hard job. We also helped with all the other cleaning that any house needs.

We had to wash and dry dishes. Since we did not have any running water, mother heated up the water in a pan and poured it in a basin to wash the dishes. We had a stool or a chair we stood on to reach the sink or table. June and I would wash and dry and fight about it along the way.

When mother did laundry down in the basement, she would not let us mess with the wringer on the washing machine. We heard horror stories about it taking a hand or an arm right in and crushing and splitting the skin, but we could poke the big stick in the rinse tub to help rinse the clothes. We also helped carry them up to the yard in a basket and hang them on the lines to dry. Later, we would go out and bring them in to the house to be sorted and put away. We learned to iron and helped mother with that too.

When I was still in grade school, mother took a job at a nursing home in Wenona, so I learned how to cook some of our basic suppers. I never did like to cook and don't to this day. Daddy had to make do with my cooking then.

Since Mother and Daddy did not have ready cash to give us for our help, they devised a method of giving us half-a-calf. That may sound odd, but they wanted us to feel we earned some money. So each year, when they sold off the calves, they would put the amount of one-half of a calf into a bank account in our name. We didn't really use that money, but we knew that it was set aside toward college.

One memory involved a dime. I took a dime from mother's purse. I was quite little, but felt so guilty that I told her. Mother took me in the back room, which was the music room, for privacy. She sat on the piano bench and set me on her lap. She thanked me for telling her and explained why it was wrong. She was so nice about it that I never forgot that incident. It was a lesson of life and living.

As we grew a little older, we learned we were marketable in other ways. One way was detasseling corn. There was a corn company in McNabb that hired kids every year to detassel corn. We earned fifty cents an hour; the work was hard and the hours were long. Mother drove us and let us off at dawn to start. In good weather, they had these huge machines that rode high above the corn. Hanging down to fit in each row were wooden planks on which the kids stood. There were probably four to five kids on each plank, and we probably did six rows with each pass down the field of the machine. Our job was to pull the tassels off the top of each stalk of corn and drop it. We had so many on a plank to insure we got all of the tassels. At dawn it is cold and wet and you freeze. Toward midmorning, your clothes started to dry out. By afternoon, it was very hot. Then by evening, it got cold again. When the ground was too muddy to get the machine through, then we had to walk. We were short and the corn stalks were really tall. So I would have to reach up and kind of bend the top down in order to pull the tassel out.

We only made fifty cents an hour, but boy, when we got a check, it was really something. For some of us, it was the first real check we had received in our name.

Another way I made money was babysitting. We had several neighbors with small children, and they would sometimes ask me to baby-sit for an evening while they went out. Again, I made fifty cents an hour. I never did like to baby-sit. I was always afraid the babies would die. I never felt that way about the older children. I do not know where that feeling came from, but I was always aware of it. I baby-sat anyway to make a little money. I never told anyone of my concerns.

During one of my high school summers, June landed me a job in Evanston, Illinois. She was attending nurses training at the Evanston Hospital and was in her ob-gyn rotation. She met this lady who had a small child and was soon to have another baby. She wanted a live-in helper to help her around the house with the kids and to baby-sit when they were gone. She agreed to have me come for the summer. That was the first time I had ever been away from home for an extended period of time.

I accepted the job and learned a lot about caring for a child and then for a baby. I also learned other things, too, as sometimes she asked me to do other household duties. One day she asked me to make her a sandwich, which I did, and I carried it in to her in my hand. She taught me that I needed to place it on a dish along with a napkin before giving it to someone. Another lesson of life learned.

Another time she asked if I knew how to make an apple pie as she had a sack full of apples to use up. I said sure. Now I had never made or cooked a pie before, but I had watched mother do it many a time. How hard could it be? Well, I made one. If I recall it was edible. That is probably the first and last pie I have ever made.

Another job that I had in a different summer was as a nursing aide. Mother was working at the Wenona Rest Home, and she needed to take time off for surgery. (A hysterectomy, I believe.) She asked the boss if I could work in her place that summer. I guess that would be considered my first real job. I was oriented by mother's friend, Sally, who worked with Mother. She was to teach me the job and oversee me at first. I did not know until years later, but mother was concerned about me seeing my first naked man. So she had discussed it with Sally in advance, and Sally was to introduce me to that part of nursing. I will say that a rest home job is an experience not gained in any other way or place.

I also learned a few other things that helped prepare me for nurses training. I learned the correct way to make a bed, take a temperature, take a B/P and pulse, and to give other types of care. I know I was proud when I started nurses training, and I was already able to do something that the other students did not yet know.

I don't recall exactly how much I was paid, but I put the money away toward nurses' training. I bought my first set of luggage with some of it. It was a hard, heavy Samsonite luggage. It was blue and I was so proud of it.

GROCERY SHOPPING AND EATING

We always bought all of our food and the supplies to run our home at a small grocery store in McNabb. The reason was that we could shop on a tab or credit there. My folks would then pay them once a year when the crop money came in. Back then, there was no such a thing as a credit or a debit card. So the store kept track of the debt for the customer. Doing it that way, along with the garden and other food generated on the farm, enabled us to always have food to eat, and we never went hungry.

We had six people in the family to feed and that took a lot of groceries. As a child, when I went shopping with mother, I was always embarrassed by the huge one or two carts full of groceries that we had. This resulted in many, many bags to carry home in the car. I would see others with only a little in their cart or only one or two bags and that bothered me. I expect we also had so much because we only went shopping once or twice a month.

We were lucky that our farm generated our meat, milk, eggs, and a lot of vegetables from the garden. We also had a strawberry patch and some blackberries.

Once a year, Daddy had someone come out from town and butcher a steer. They prepared the meat in various ways and packaged it for freezing. We had a locker in the meat locker in Lostant where we stored it. When I went with mother in to pick up meat, I was always afraid of that huge door—afraid that we would get stuck inside. It never happened, but my imagination said it could have.

We only had meat on special occasions. On Sunday, mother tried to usually have a meat dish. Also, if we had company we would have meat. We had our own chickens to supplement our diet on special occasions.

Daddy always took the time to plant a garden. Usually, he would plow a section in the field, and we would plant sweet corn, tomatoes, green onions, potatoes, radishes, and other things. The garden always grew well along with the weeds, which nobody had time to pull. I probably helped in the planting, but once it filled up with weeds, I would not go in the garden because we had those huge black and yellow spiders that made a big web across a corn row or between plants. I also did not like to pick the vegetables for the same reason.

Down at the bend in our lane, we had a strawberry patch that came back every year. When they ripened, we would get strawberry shortcake once in a while with real whipped cream. Boy was that a treat!

We also had a few blackberry vines behind the chicken house that we would pick and just eat. They were great too.

Mother canned every year. She mostly canned tomatoes. We would have a big production of boiling water and jars and lids being sterilized. Then, of course, were the peeling of the tomatoes and cooking them and putting them up. When all was finished, we stored them in the basement. Mother used the canned tomatoes all year long and added them to many dishes. I loved to eat a ripe tomato with sugar and still do.

Our daily diet was mainly beans, potatoes, and eggs. We had pork and beans from the store, potatoes from the garden or from the store, and eggs from our chickens. We ate this probably six out of seven days a week. Mother would boil the potatoes for one meal and then fry the left over for the next meal.

For breakfast we usually had cold cereal and milk. Once in a while, Mother would cook oatmeal, or she would make pancakes or French toast. Those times were always special. I loved any of those. One rule was that all was cooked before anyone started eating so we could all sit down together and enjoy the meal.

For lunches at school, we took baloney sandwiches or peanut butter and jelly sandwiches. Sometimes a piece of fruit. Sometimes cookies that mother bought. The school had these small cartons of milk for two cents. I loved it when I had two cents and could get a chocolate milk. Chocolate in any form has been my favorite all of my life.

I would be remiss if I did not mention ice cream. I loved it. In fact, we all did, but we got it only on special occasions, such as for a birthday party or if company came over.

There was a girl in my class who I grew up with named Janice. We would sometimes have a chance to play together. I loved it when I had a chance to go to her house. She was able to go to the freezer anytime she liked and get ice cream for us. I thought that was so neat and was so jealous of that freedom.

OLD CARS

Mother and Daddy always drove old cars, because they could never afford to buy a new one. It was the same way with the tractor and farm machinery. Daddy became very adept at fixing the cars and the machinery to keep them running.

As a child, I guess I was concerned about looks

and was very aware that we drove old cars while my friends and relatives had new cars. I remember this one old blue Nash that looked like an upside-down bathtub. When we had to go to a school function, I always hoped no one would see me getting out of it. Lostant is such a small town that everybody knew what car belonged to whom anyway.

Daddy had a big gas tank up on high legs that we used to fill our car from. A tanker truck came every so often and filled it up, so we never had to go to a regular gas station in town. This next incident really belongs in my adult section of the book, but it fits well here so I will include it.

When I graduated from nurses' training, I bought a used 1960 Ford Fairlane. This was my first car. I bought it in Chicago. I believe that my brother, John, helped me to choose a good car. The first time I went to a gas station my friend and old roommate, Bonnie, was with me. Back then, they did not have self-serve, so this young man came out and filled up my car. I paid for it and then tipped him. Bonnie got all excited and went and took the tip away. I learned another life lesson.

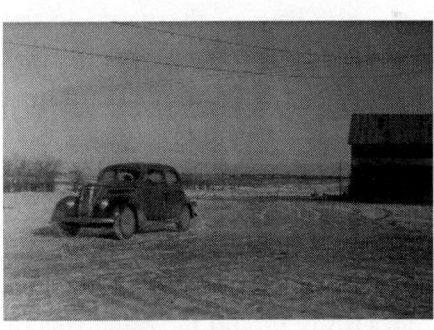

THE BARN AND HAYING SEASON

The barn was a place of many mysteries and fun. As a child, I always thought it huge, but seeing it in later life I realized it was not as big as I remembered.

The first section of the barn was the area to milk the cow. The next was the pony stall. Behind this area was a walkway, and then behind that were other stalls.

The other section of the barn was for hay storage, which included the hay mows. We had big double doors on either side of the barn that opened up so Daddy could drive the tractor and hay rack into the center. Above, on both sides, was the hay mow. There was also a smaller room on the bottom level where hay was stored.

There was a door in one end of the mow. It opened so the pulley system could hook up to the tractor outside. Across the roof of the barn, on the inside, was the rope and pulley arrangement. This was the way we got the bales up into the hay mow. There were four huge hooks that dropped down to the hay rack. Daddy would have eight bales stacked, and he fastened these hooks into the lower bales of this stack. The tractor then slowly pulled the load up until it swung across to where it needed to be dropped in the mow. Daddy would have the tractor halted and pull a rope, which released the bales in a jumble. We would pull them aside and stack them in the hay mow. A person always had to be careful, as sometimes a hook came loose and a bale could drop back to the rack or drop in the mow before you were ready for it.

This was repeated over and over, rack after rack, until the mows were as full as possible. If we still had more bales, we would stack them outside—sometimes next to the barn, sometimes in a small area in the cow pasture. We used the hay all year especially in the winter months to feed the livestock. We occasionally sold some.

Straw, which was baled from the stalk after the harvest of oats, was stacked too. It was used as bedding for the livestock in the barn and for the chickens in the chicken house. We also sold some of this from time to time.

I sort of got the cart before the horse here and told you about the final process of the haying season. Now let me tell you about haying itself.

This was the best season of the year. Earlier in the year, Daddy would plant the clover. Just a side note, when the clover was flowering, you could pick the little purple ends of the flower and suck on them—just as sweet as honey. I guess that is why the bees liked it so much.

When the clover was ready for cutting, Daddy would use the big mower to cut it. Then he would use the rake that curled the cuttings into rows. He would then come along with the baler and bale the hay. The baler processed the hay so that twine went around each bale in two places. Then the bailer spit the bale out on the ground.

The big factor in haying was to do the whole

process from cutting, to baling, to picking up the bales, to storing them before it rained—always important every year. I loved to help with any of the haying process that I could. Mostly I walked along the rack and threw the bales up on the rack. I was a strong child to be able to do that. Sometimes I rode on the rack and stacked the bales. Sometimes, I was in the hay mow stacking bales.

Many times Daddy hired help to get it all done in a timely manner. I always felt so big because I could work with all these guys and do a good job. I felt proud that they talked to me and treated me like an adult.

Part of my haying experience was putting up hay on Grandma's farm. There were several incidents that happened there, which I will never forget.

One time I was walking on the ground throwing bales up on the rack. I picked up this bale, and there was a nest of bees beneath it. These were the big black and yellow bumblebees. They swarmed, and I started running with them chasing me. In the middle of a hay field, there is absolutely no place to go for shelter. I was about halfway up the field from the car at the end. I ran as fast as I could and got in the car. I was stung five times. Outside of the normal pain of the bee stings, I was okay.

Another year, in that same field, I was again throwing bales onto the rack and was at the end of the field along the fence line. I found three baby skunks. Now, since I always wanted a skunk for a pet, I thought I had hit the jackpot. I knew I had to finish haying for the day before I could deal with them, so I put them behind a bale to hold them until later. No parent skunks were around, so they were probably orphaned.

When we were about three-fourths of the way down the field from that fence, I saw my grandmother's two dogs racing across the field between our field and the house. I started running back toward the babies, too, but the dogs were faster and got there first. By the time I arrived, the dogs had killed them all. I was heartbroken, but I kind of think Mother and Daddy were probably relieved.

SCHOOL AND EDUCATION

When John and June first went to school, they attended a one-room school house in the country not too far from where we lived. Yet by the time I started school, it was held in Lostant. It was a combination of grade school and high school in one two-story building. Later before I reached the 7th grade, they added onto this building with more classrooms, a music room, and a shop.

Mother and Daddy always imparted to us the importance of a good education. Before we went to school, Mother did some teaching in phonics and reading and math. After the second grade, mother felt that I was falling behind, so she bought some home study books. All that summer, I had to do lessons and study with her. It must have helped, because after that, I kept up fine in all my classes.

During that time, I was having a lot of fun on the playground during recess. They had these gliders that were attached to a tall metal pole. Each glider hung down on a chain, and it had an upper and lower handle you held onto. You went around and around, running and swinging. I loved to play on this, and mother said that sometimes the bigger kids would knock me off, but I always wanted back on. She said I used to come home all dirty and messy. I remember them well, along with the swings and other playground equipment.

We also had to play in sports—outside in the good weather and in the gym when it was bad. Softball was always a problem for me. I was never any good at it. I could not hit the ball well, and I was afraid to catch it. Every time we played, they would choose two captains. Then these captains would choose the team, alternating with each other in picking. I hated it because I would always be last or next to last. To be picked last made me feel bad, unwanted, and unliked. I did a little better in basketball, but not so well in volleyball. I guess that is enough said about sports.

Education was the main emphasis of school. I received good grades, but not wonderful. I brought my studies home, but did not study as hard as June did. I relished my time out on the farm. However, I took the classes I needed to graduate and to be prepared as much as possible for nurses' training.

In high school, our principal, Mr. Graber, taught geometry. I made a mistake and then made the same mistake again another time. He said, "Anyone can make a mistake once, only a fool does it twice." Another life lesson learned.

In high school, a group of us sold concession at the boys' basketball games. I enjoyed doing that. I felt included.

Our high school graduating class only had thirteen students. So you can believe that we knew all the students in the whole high school. I was never popular and never dated even though I did have a crush on one boy. He never knew it. I was always shy. My main socialization probably happened through the church groups.

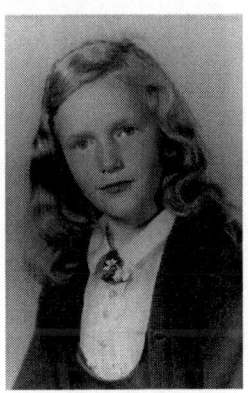
1954 age 11

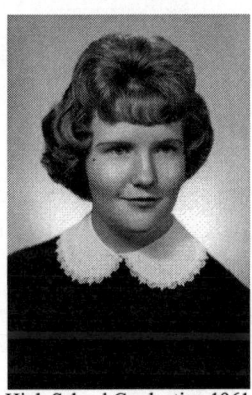
High School Graduation 1961

CLOTHES AND HAIR

At home, on the farm, I always wore hand-me-downs, usually slacks or jeans and a top. Never anything fancy and often they had holes or shaggy spots. That never bothered me as we worked and played hard in these clothes. We were never allowed to wear shorts all the time I was at home, and after I left home, I used to feel guilty whenever I wore shorts around my parents.

When I was small, I never paid attention to what mother dressed me in to go to school. I was not very careful of my clothes. I played hard, but we knew that we had to change when we got home to keep our school clothes nice.

As I got older, in grade school and in high school, I began to become more concerned about my clothes. I was always so excited when mother would take us shopping before school started each year. We would each get a certain number of outfits. For the girls, we had to wear skirts or dresses. We even looked like young ladies.

Around about 6th or 7th grade, I got this one skirt I truly loved and I wanted to wear it all the time. That lasted until the girls at school started to tease me. Another life lesson learned.

Mother made sure June and I learned to iron. Back then, everything had to be ironed. So we learned to do our own and also to be able to help out with the other household ironing. That has always held me in good stead the rest of my life.

Mother made sure we had special outfits for

special occasions, such as Easter or a special school function. We always got a pretty Easter dress and new white shoes and maybe a bonnet of some kind. We wore this to church on Easter Sunday and then for special things. I always felt so pretty.

Mother always wanted our hair to look nice, and both June and I had long hair. Junes was brown and mine was blonde. When we were little she fixed it in banana curls for both of us. Nobody else in church had these and I always felt special and pretty and proud. Looking back, I don't understand how mother ever had the time to do all the things she did for all of us. She gave each one of us pride in ourselves and a sense of worth.

One time in high school June invited me up to her hospital in Evanston for a date. This was a big adventure for me. Mother realized I needed a special dress and bought me this beautiful blue sheath. The first grown up dress or sheath I ever had. I got a nice pair of heels and a purse. At this time, June was dating a Navy guy named Joe, and I was going to date his buddy. We had a good time, but I really don't remember the details.

Mother tried to make us feel special when things like that arose and she succeeded.

FUN TIMES

We had so many fun times when we were growing up. Many of the times we created for ourselves. Some things Mother and Daddy created, and we enjoyed them immensely.

When I was young, I was always playing bookstore. I could lose hours doing this. I would go around the house finding all the magazines and periodicals that came in the mail. I would cart them upstairs and lay them out on the bed and pretend to sell them. This was all okay, but I bet Mother and Daddy often wondered where all their reading material went as soon as it came in the house.

Another thing we did in the summer was to take an old blanket and put it over the clothesline outside. We spread it out and used it for a tent. We had flashlights and eats. It was fun.

Another thing that mother loved to do with us kids was hunt for Indian Beads. We would go out and sit in the gravel road. Any little rock that had a hole through it qualified. We also found an occasional piece of petrified wood. We kept our collection in an old, small tin box. We loved to do this and will never forget it. We still have that collection.

Easter was always a great time for the family. As I mentioned before, we usually had a new dress to wear. Mother always painted Easter eggs and let us help when we were old enough to know about the fable of the Easter bunny. Mother and Daddy would hide the eggs all over the yard in good weather or in the house if the weather was bad.

The fourth of July was always a fun time for our family. We got sparklers and caps for our cap guns. We also got a few small fireworks, but most of the fun was our yearly trip to Henry, where professional fireworks were held every year. All the people sat on blankets and chairs on one side of the river, and the fireworks were shot off from the other side. Before the fireworks was a carnival on our side of the river. If I was lucky, I got cotton candy. We always got bit up by mosquitoes, and it was hot and humid in July. Still, to kids, none of that seemed to matter. It was a time to look forward too and definitely to remember.

At Halloween, sometimes, we had a party at our house. Usually it was for the church group kids or the MYF. Daddy would go all out for this party. He would build a big stack of wood for a bonfire in the middle of our barnyard. In good weather, he would have bales of hay a distance from it for us to sit on. In bad weather, he cleared out the machine shed and put the bales of hay in there. We roasted hot dogs and marshmallows. Then when it got nice and dark, he would start telling ghost stories. We would pass around things in the dark like peeled grapes and say they were eyeballs. Mother, of course, was there, too, but I think Daddy did most of it. All the kids loved it.

Another outing that we all really loved was going to a movie in town on Saturday evenings. We usually went to Streator. We saw cowboy movies featuring Tom Mix or Roy Rogers or Gene Autry or Hopalong Cassidy, and many others. Mother would stop at the Rexall Drug store first and buy ten cents worth of M&Ms. (You must have gotten more then.)

Then she would divide them up between the four of us. Of course, mine were all gone before the movie started. Robert used to save his and take them home and put them in his dresser drawer. That bothered me to no end, and I was known to bargain for them.

Another family outing that we always looked forward to was going to the Springfield State Fair. This was 100 miles away and provided a big time for us. Mother always packed a picnic lunch as it was too expensive to eat there. We would all meet back at the car at a certain time for lunch. As we got older, we were allowed to go together to the fair and see the sights.

One incident I remember is the time I was with Johnny, and we were seeing the fair. Several other kids started picking on me, and Johnny stood up for me and made them quit. I never forgot that.

Mother and Daddy would usually give us a quarter that we could spend on a ride or on a treat or however we wanted. The only rule was, if we got cotton candy it had to be at the end of the day so we were not sticky all day.

The fair had all kinds of animals and farm machinery to see. They gave away things like yard sticks, and we always got some there. It was an all day trip, and I expect we slept most of the way home.

Another area of great enjoyment for all of us was reading. We were all encouraged to read, and when we were little, and even older, mother would read to us. We had this one big Bible that had the prettiest green-and orange-toned pictures in it. Mother brought us up on all the stories of the Bible. Another book that we all loved was *Sugar Loaf Mountain*.

Grandma gave us lots of books. She also gave a lot of books to the library at school. She herself was a very learned woman and liked to read. She gave us many novels, and also many condensed Reader's Digest books. We had a small, walk-in closet in the upstairs hallway where we put all the books. It was our own private library.

Several of the books I loved as a child were, *My Friend Flicka*, *Green Grass of Wyoming*, *Thunderhead*, and *The Yellow Room*. Those first three were a series, and I read them over and over again. The last one was a mystery, which I also read many times. In fact, just recently, June came across all of those except "Thunderhead" and sent them to me. So now I have them.

Mother ordered us subscriptions to two comic books, which came every month. We all loved them and waited for them to arrive. These featured Little Lulu and Donald Duck. Then one time, our cousin, Louie, gave us boxes of his comics—500 in all. We read and reread and loved them to tatters.

Mother and Daddy worked hard on the farm and never had time for trips or vacations. I only remember them taking us on one vacation. It was to the Wisconsin Dells. I especially remember the boat ride we had with big, odd-shaped rocks on either side of the river. On another weekend trip, I recall staying at the Plantation Hotel in Chicago. That was my first hotel experience. That night we attended the Grand Old Opera in downtown Chicago.

Other times that we all had lots of fun was when family came to visit, or we would go to their homes to visit. Our cousins were around our age, and we all played together and had a great time. Sometimes we had family reunions, and people came from other states. We were able to keep track of most of the family this way. We still have reunions every few years.

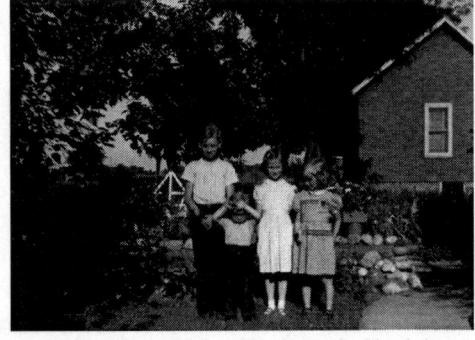
John, Robert, June, and myself in front of a friends house.

DOCTORS AND BEING SICK

Thankfully, we were not sick that much. We had the usual childhood diseases, including measles, mumps, whooping cough, chicken pox, etc. We weathered through all of them. I am sure they were all harder on Mother than anyone else.

Mother always seemed to have Sulfa. I expect she got it from the doctor, but for Mother that was the drug of choice. I always had trouble swallowing a pill, even one broken up. So mother would mash it in a spoon and mix it with water. Talk about horrible. I can taste it to this day. When she was holding it for me or watching me, I had to take it and then immediately eat something to wash it down. If she was not watching, our sink drain got a hefty dose of Sulfa every now and again.

The other thing Mother gave us when we were sick was tea and toast. I never cared for it then nor do I drink tea today.

In the winter, when snow was heavy, Daddy sometimes had to walk clear to the neighbor's house to call the doctor. This was probably 1 to 1½ miles across the fields. Sometimes the doctor came out to the house; otherwise we saw him in the office in Tonica.

Once when I was playing down in the pig lot by the well, I was on an old watering bin and I jumped off. I jumped right onto a board with a rusty nail. I yelled and screamed until Robert came, and then he got Mother. She took me immediately to the doctor for a tetanus shot.

When Robert was quite young, they realized he definitely had a vision problem. We had to go clear to Bloomington to see an eye doctor. He got glasses. Well, let me tell you, I became blind as a bat. I was so jealous of Robert's glasses. Mother realized what was going on and handled it very well. Even though it probably cost money, she took me to see the eye doctor too. Of course, he found nothing wrong and explained all this to me. That soothed my feelings, and I was able to accept it all.

THE HOUSE

I have mentioned a little about the house, but wish to bring out a few other things. As I said it was a white two-story building. Upstairs were four fairly large bedrooms, compared with bedrooms in homes today. Mother and Daddy had one room, John and Robert had another, and June and I shared a room. The 4th room was used for a guest room, for storage, and etc.

All the windows of the house had these rope pulley arrangements on the sides that let you slide the window up and down. Sometimes that was broke, and we used a stick to prop it up. The other thing I remember about the windows was the build up of frost and ice on the inside window and sill during the winter. The window screens usually had holes or tears in them, so we had plenty of flies around during the summer months.

We had wallpaper throughout the house, and one time we even had a man out to hang wallpaper. I found this process interesting to watch. He drank ginger ale.

The upstairs floors were plain wood, but downstairs we had linoleum and carpet. We had a large area carpet in the parlor. The path through the middle was rather threadbare. The linoleum was the same way. Many parts were worn through the design, down to the black color of the backing.

The bottom floor was laid out with the kitchen first coming in from the small porch on the front of the house. It contained an enamel topped table with a set of six wooden, white-chipped chairs. The table had two leaves on the ends that you could pull up to provide additional places for people to sit. We had a large, long sink with a pump, which you pumped for non-drinking water. We used this water for cleaning and so on. We had a propane gas stove for cooking and also a round, potbelly wood-burning stove for heating that room. There was a pantry off to one side to help with storage. Then of course, there was the refrigerator.

The next room to the left from the back door entrance was the living room. We had an oil stove in that room for heat. We had a desk and also a long formal table with 6–8 chairs. Mother used this table when we had company. She kept padding on it so it would not get scratched. She also wrapped the table legs as long as there were young children running around. One thing this table was used for was for a catch-all. Everybody laid stuff on it, so if we had company we had to clean it all off.

The next room was the parlor. We were not allowed to use this room except when we had company. We all obeyed this rule. Mother and Daddy had a beautiful couch and chair of a brown material that I just loved. Robert now has it in his home, and I am so glad he has it. They also had a buffet, which mother kept really nice. She had pretty things setting on top. She kept keepsakes and pictures inside. She also set the formal dining chairs around this room. She had small tables and knickknack shelves. She was very proud of her furniture and said we had to be careful of it because it had to last a lifetime. It did, plus years after they have passed. She said when they were first married Daddy took her shopping, and they picked out all these beautiful things.

The next room was the music room. We had a big upright piano and bench, music stands, instruments, and music cabinets. The parlor and music room did not have any heat of their own, so we sometimes shut the doors in the winter to conserve heat for the rest of the house.

All the buildings on the farm, including the house, were white except the barn which was red. I don't really remember any painting ever being done on any of the buildings, but it may have happened.

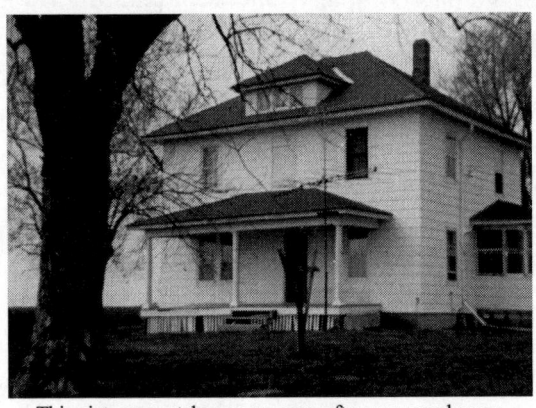

This picture was taken many years after we moved away.

NO—NO—NONE

Our farm was fairly primitive in amenities. As you gathered from past chapters, we did not have any indoor plumbing. We carried all of our drinking water from the pony lot well. We had to heat all water that needed to be warm or hot water. We had a big enamel pan that we used to heat water on the stove. We all took our baths on the weekend and often used the same bathwater for more than one person. We had a big, round galvanized tub that mother set down in the basement near the end of the stairs in the summer. In the winter, she set that same tub in the middle of the kitchen near the potbelly stove. Of course, that inhibited people from entering or leaving the house by the front door. I knew I was a big girl when the males could not walk through the room anymore.

  Also, in the summer, we had a shower of sorts. Daddy rigged a radiator behind the garage in the corner made by the garage and the machine shed. It had a spigot you could stand under for the water. You had to do a little dance to get all the soap rinsed off. It was sun heated. Daddy had to get up there and pour the water in from time to time. Of course, you had to remember to take your towel and clean clothes out with you. It was not unheard of for someone partially dressed to be coming across the barnyard and have some car drive up the lane.

  When June and I were small, mother would wash our hair in the long kitchen sink. She would place me on the back of the ironing board with my hair hanging down in the sink and then she would pour warm water over it with a pan for the washing and the rinsing. This was a good way to keep the soap out of our eyes as well.

  With no central heat or air conditioning, the

stoves in the kitchen and in the front room provided all of our heat. The upstairs bedrooms each had a register in the floor in which some of the heat floated up from the downstairs. Basically, it was very cold upstairs in the winter, and we covered up well at night. On real cold mornings, many is the time we grabbed our clothes and ran down to dress behind the stove in the living room.

In the summer, we opened the windows for air circulation, and sometimes it was very hot, especially in the upstairs at night. As kids, we did not know anything else and were okay with it all. That was just the way it was.

We also did not have a telephone, so we never grew up on the phone as kids do today. If it was an important matter, Mother or Daddy went over to the neighbors' house to use their phone. Our neighbors were always very gracious about helping out.

Another item we never had was a television. That was probably for the best. That is why we loved to read and why I loved the outdoors so much. Here again, we really did not realize we were missing anything. The only time I got to see TV was on the occasion when I might visit my girlfriend at her house. Even then, we seldom watched TV. We had so many other things to do on her farm or in her house.

All in all, we did not realize we were missing out on all these things. We all learned fortitude and to be able to handle difficult situations. It gave us a "can-do" outlook on life.

PETS OF ALL KINDS

I have loved animals all of my life and have usually had pets of one kind or another. As a child, I had pets my grandmother gave me or any wild animal I could catch and keep. I want to tell you about various pets I had as a child and may not list them in order, but they were all special to me.

Rex was my dog. Grandma gave him to me. He was a mutt—sort of a small collie mix. I loved Rex. He was just a little puppy, and I would take him to the barn and teach him to come and do what I asked. Rex was my constant companion when I was outside. Mother and Daddy would never allow a dog or cat in the house, so Rex lived outside or in the barn. When I went out to explore the farm and the pig lot, Rex was always with me. He came along when I was on the pony and helped to bring the cattle home. One day when I was on foot up in the cow pasture, this black and white milk cow started after me. Rex ran between me and the cow, diverting her while I crawled under a fence. Rex may have saved me from a lot of hurt that day. Rex caught some of his own food, such as rabbits. In fact, we did not buy dog food but did give him table scraps. He thrived just the same. We did not know it was bad to give a dog chicken bones. I am sure Rex ate lots of them with no problem.

Later I will talk about moving to the new house, but when we did Rex went with us. I left for nurses training, and once when I came home for a visit, Rex was not there. Mother told me that he had disappeared. She said that when I left he would not eat right and seemed lost without me. Later Daddy did find his body in the ditch by the road, probably hit by a car. On the old farm, we were so far away from the roads. The new house was right on a well-traveled road. It was hard to get over the loss of Rex.

Now back to the old farm. Grandma also gave me a yellow cat. It was a long-hair angora and she was my cat. Again, the cat (can't remember its name) lived in the barn. I expect Daddy gave it milk every morning while milking. Sometimes, Mother or Daddy would drive the car down the lane to meet the bus and give us a ride home. Mother said that cat would watch every day for the bus to show at the end of the lane. Then it ran down to the end of the barnyard and followed the car back to the house, just so I could play with it. I do not really recall what happened to that cat.

We also had lots of barn cats from time to time that always stayed in or around the barn. They hunted for mice and rats and rabbits. They had their babies in the barn, usually in the hay mow somewhere. It was always great fun to search the barn when we knew kittens were born. We would find them and play with them down there. One time I was so hurt because I went down to play with them and found their heads missing. Mother said an old tom cat probably did that. I put them all in a sack and took them to my special tree in the pig lot. We usually had kittens born every year in the barn.

Another family pet was Chip. This was a sparrow that mother raised. It had fallen out of a nest. At first it was fed bread and milk. Later we kept it in a bird cage in the house. Chip was able to fly all around the house. Chip would play hide-and-seek and would take frosting or mints from your fingers and then kiss you on the lips to thank you for it. Chip was so tame and so loved. I think Chip probably died of old age.

Another pet we had was this beautiful, red banty rooster. June's art teacher gave him to her, and she brought him home to live on the farm. This banty was an ornery little thing. It would be scratching around in the yard and see you coming up the sidewalk. It would wait for you to pass and then run up behind you and attack your legs. If you turned around, it was nonchalantly scratching around again until you turned back, then it would attack you. It had great fun doing that. We always took it to the barn to sleep at night. So at dusk, it would jump up on the front windowsill to await someone to come out and carry it to the barn. We would take it to the barn, and if someone had not closed all the doors of the barn, it would get out and run back up to the house and jump up on the windowsill again and wait for a trip back to the barn. Sometimes we would bring it in the house and hold it on our laps in front of the oil stove. It loved that. During the day, it ran all over wherever it felt like.

Joe was a wild crow. I was up in the top of the corn crib once and found Joe. His wing was injured and he could not fly. Of course, I brought him up to the house to keep. Well, Joe was a big bird and made big messes and not exactly a house bird. We had this old wooden clothes rack. Mother set it up on the side of the front porch with papers under it, and that is where Joe lived for the summer. Yet in the winter, it was too cold on the porch so mother moved him out to live in the chicken house. Joe loved people and always wanted to be around people. He put up with living with the chickens but had to protect himself. The chickens did not like this bird running around. (Joe never did fly—only ran on the ground.) The chickens would peck at him as he went past, and he lost most of his tail feathers. Joe was also sneaky. When the chickens went to sleep on the roost, Joe would sort of worm his way in between to keep warm. Joe would make the funniest sounds, and we always thought he was trying to talk. Of course, I loved Joe and he was with us a number of years. One eve when we went out to lock up the hen house, Joe was not there. We never knew what happened to him.

  I captured this ground squirrel once. I was down in the pony lot, and there was this real long pipe laying on the ground, and I saw the squirrel go in one end. Well, I upended the pipe, then somehow put a bucket over that end, withdrew the pipe, and I had a squirrel. Of course, I took it to the house. We had this big, old cage out on the long porch on the side of the house. I fixed it all up with straw and food and water. I tried to tame it and love it. I had to wear heavy gloves whenever I caught it as it would bite me. After a few months, I realized I was never going to tame this pet, so I let it loose. Nice try though.

This Country Girl

Robert and I had a white rat that Johnny brought home from college. He had a job working with white rats in a research lab. He brought one home and of course, I loved it. We had a smaller cage inside the house that we rigged up on two poles in a box so that the droppings dropped into the lower box. I could pick up this rat and play with it as much as I wanted. I used to tease my aunt Dolores with it as she did not like it. Thinking back, it was not a nice thing to do. I also teased her with a dead snake once. I had this bull snake and laid it across the steps leading down from the front porch. Then when she started coming out, I wiggled it. That was not nice either.

We occasionally had stray dogs that people would drop off in our lane, and they would wander up to the barnyard. Some stayed and some were bad. One dog started killing our chickens, so Daddy had to shoot it. Some of them just left on their own.

We had our share of white bunnies. We had this long rabbit hutch that had a little house at one end and then the rest was made out of wire and wood. When the bunnies got older, they could run around the farm and some disappeared. Daddy always thought hunters got some.

One time we had some Easter ducklings that we kept in this same rabbit hutch as the rabbits. We made a mistake. Every night we put the little ducks inside the small house and put several bricks in the doorway so nothing could get at them during the night. We were supposed to remove the bricks every morning so they could run around the enclosure.

Well, one day we forgot and went to church. It was a warm day. By the time we found them, they had died. We learned a hard lesson that day. I guess some of these lessons taught us responsibility.

One year in the fall, mother found this robin with an injured wing. She brought it in the house and fixed the wing. However, by the time it had healed and the bird could fly, winter had set in and all the robins were gone. So she put papers down on the floor, and the bird set on the clotheslines across the front room and flew around the room all winter long. Then when spring came, she turned the bird out and it took off.

Our house had a long porch on one side. At the top of the support columns is where the swallows would build their nests. They built mud nests. They would have their babies, and we could watch the whole process from our windows. We watched the babies grow and learn to fly. They came back every year to that porch.

John had a calf called Levi. I believe he raised it as a 4-H project. It lived with the other cattle and was a big Black Angus. Levi grew quite big, and John planned to sell him and use the money for college. Nevertheless, one day Levi did not come home with the rest of the cattle. So John went looking for him. He found him dead in the spring pasture down by the spring. I do not believe they ever found out why Levi died. If I remember rightly, Mother and Daddy gave John another calf to sell, but it was not the same. We all were blue for what happened to Levi.

Several other stories don't involve pets, but I thought were interesting—concerning a skunk, a calf, and an opossum.

We had the big tin can and bottle pile in back of the house, off to the right in a vacant lot. We continually added cans and bottles and non-burnable items to it. The skunks liked to forage in it for food. One night we were looking out the front window, and this skunk was coming up the sidewalk with a jar on its head. Daddy went out to deal with it. I do not know the end result, whether he ended up shooting it or if he got the jar off and let it go.

We had a lot of hay stacked in a part of the cow lot. Sometimes the cattle would come up to eat in the area. I had a rope and I made a big circle at one end, which I put next to the hay. The other end I would hold outside the fence. My desire was for a calf to step in the rope, and I would pull it tight and catch him. I did this many a day, but never did catch one. I don't know what would have happened if I did.

As I have mentioned, I explored all over the farm. Once I was in a field, up almost as far away from the house as I could get, and I found this big opossum. I thought it was dead, but boy that was a great find. I took it by the tail, and since it was way too heavy for me to carry, I had to drag it. I drug it all the way home under fences and everything. When I got it home, Daddy said it was still alive and was just playing possum, so he took it and turned it loose.

Mother and Daddy put up with a lot from all of my animals. They never tried to tell me not to catch them. They always helped me get places ready for them to live and supported me that way. That was truly a wonderful part of childhood.

LEAVING THE FARM

Mother and Daddy decided to move off the farm and into the Lyons' house on the other side of Lostant. They decided to just live in the house and farm only Grandma's farm, which was down the same road. It was an 80-acre farm.

We moved in 1959, when I was in my second year of high school. This was a very traumatic move for me. Everything I loved was at the old farm. I think I really gave up my childhood at that point.

I still helped out with the farm work and haying at Grandma's, but it was never the same. Our new house was also a two-story. It had more amenities. We had an indoor bathroom, which was really a plus. It had running water, hot and cold, and a big bathtub you could soak in if you could keep the bathroom long enough. I think Johnny was away to college by this time, so that left the five of us.

We also had a phone. It was one of these old, tall crank phones where you spoke into the mouthpiece on the front and held the earpiece to your ear. It was rather high on the wall, and short people used a chair. It was a party line, and you had a special set of rings to signify your house. You had to also remember that anyone along the line could listen in.

None of us were much for using the phone by this time anyway.

We still did not have a TV.

The farmland around this house was farmed by the Lyons. There were several out buildings they used. The only redeeming feature this farm had was an old well. It was way up in the middle of the field. It was a small oasis of trees, weeds, and junk. The old well was boarded up so no person or animal would fall in. This place was the only sanctuary I had, where I could get away.

We did not have a half-mile lane anymore, so we just walked a short distance to the road to get on the school bus.

Mother and Daddy lived at this house after I left home. Later on, in 1966, they ended up moving to Grandma's house to live, once she moved to Granville, Illinois.

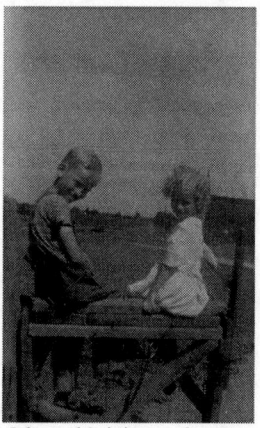

John and I sitting on the gate.

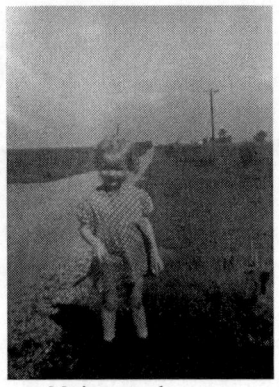
Me in my early years.

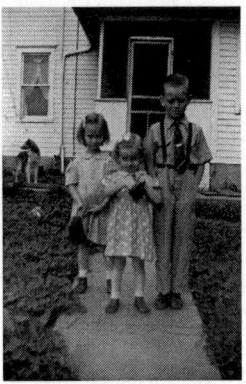
June, myself, and John in front of the house.

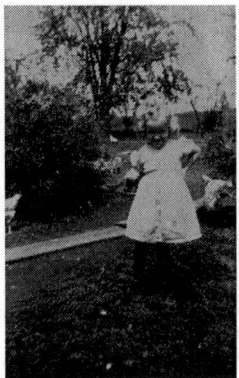
Me in my early years.

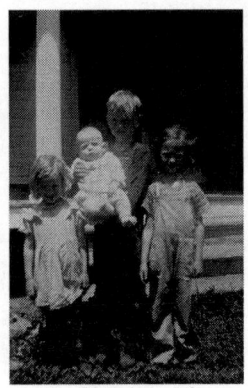
Myself, Robert, John, and June.

Chapter Two - Nurses' Training

STUDY AND WORK

All of the time we were growing up, Mother instilled in all of us the idea that we should go to college. She always said we needed to get away from Lostant and home and make something of ourselves.

John, the oldest, was the first to go. He went to Kendall College in Chicago.

Robert, the youngest, also went to college in his turn.

June—Well, Mother always wanted both her daughters to become nurses. Mother had attended nurses' training, but decided to drop out after 15 months, to get married and raise a family, as she was getting older. Mother had already attended a few years in college before she entered nurses' training. Mother really wanted her girls to become nurses. She also felt that it would give us a good way to support ourselves.

June went to the Evanston Hospital School of Nursing in Evanston, Illinois, near Chicago. She is two years older than I am, so she was two years into her training when I started. Both of our programs were three-year diploma programs.

I went to nurses training from the fall of 1961

to the fall of 1964. I chose Illinois Masonic Hospital School of Nursing in Chicago, mainly because of cost. It was less expensive, and I had received an Eastern Star Scholarship and a Kiwanis Club Scholarship that helped to cover the cost of this three-year diploma program.

We lived in a dormitory, and I had a roommate, Bonnie. We got along fine.

I found out that I needed to study all of the time. A three-year diploma program amounts to attending classes part of the day and working in the hospital part of the day. As you get further along, they give you more responsibility in the hospital wards, and often you are in charge for a shift. You may do days, evenings, or the night shift. You do all your studying around your class and work schedule. Thus I did not find much time for playing or dating.

I knew after I had been there three months that I really did not want to be a nurse, but I did it and I did it very well. I made good grades and did my work thoroughly, to the best of my ability. I think that happened for two reasons. One, I did not want to let Mother and Daddy down. They had inspired me so much and wanted so much for me to do well. The other reason was I could do no less than June. She was making good grades and doing very well, so I had to too. I carried my idea of excellence all through school and through my life.

As students, our first triumph was to make it to capping. This is the ceremony where they give you your nurse's cap, and you can wear it proudly after that. Some of our students did not make it that far, so I felt good that I was doing well.

After my first year at school, the freshman class had to sing for the graduating seniors at their graduation ceremony. This ceremony was held in this big, old hall with a lower level where the graduating class and all the guests sat. It also had a balcony where the freshman class sat to sing. At one point in the ceremony, they said they were going to honor the freshman of the year who was chosen by the faculty. Well, they called me. I was so surprised and excited; out of seventy-some students, I was the one chosen. That was really an honor.

I want to relate a few interesting stories and details about nurses' training.

When we first started classes, we had an anatomy class taught by this male teacher who was rumored to be very tough and who never gave a 100 percent grade. I remember he had only one hand. The other was a stump that he used like a hand, all of the time.

One of our first major tests was called a "bone practicum." There are over 200 bones in the body, and he demanded that you learn each one's name—where it was located in the body and also the names of various facets of the bones.

I made a complete list and memorized it. When I lay down to sleep, I would rehearse the whole list every night.

The day came for the testing. It was an oral test. So when he called me in, I was very confident.

He asked me a number of different questions. I got them all right. Then he asked me a question that we had not yet studied. By doing this, he was able to give me a 99 percent so he could keep his record. I never forgot that.

We had various rotations in which we learned about portions of nursing, such as obstetrics or pediatrics. We had classes on the subject at the same time we worked on that particular ward in the hospital. Medical-surgical nursing was a big section, and we did a lot of work on the med-surg wards at various times all throughout our schooling.

We learned all aspects of each rotation—from caring for patients' physical needs such as bed baths, ambulating the patients, giving them their medications, changing intravenous feedings, putting down nasal-gastric tubes, inserting catheters, caring for and dressing wounds, and operating various equipment or machines hooked up to the patients. There are far too many things to list them all, but this is an idea of what we learned and did.

Medication back then was not the individually prepackaged pills as they use now. We had bottles of medicine sent up by the pharmacy in a patient's name that we kept in the medication room. When a person was assigned to medications, they put up the medications for the whole ward. We had a Cardex, with all the patients medications listed and a separate small card for each medication. You first checked this card against the Cardex. The Cardex was updated from the doctor's orders. You set up each patient's medications in a cup and placed the cards in a slot for that cup. Then you went on to the next patient's medication. Finally, you passed the medications to the patients on the whole floor. This was all quite time consuming. You also had various other times that an individual patient might receive medications so you had to keep track of that as well. You kept careful track of the narcotics and pain medications used. You also had to account for each narcotic in a log. These had to be counted at the end of each shift jointly by two nurses. You also kept track of intravenous fluids and the IV medications and changed the IVs or restarted them as needed. It depended on your assignment as to whether you did the medications for the whole ward or if you were to do them only for the particular patients with whom you were assigned to work with that day. We were given experience in doing it both ways. Both ways included charting of all the medications, the patients acceptance of the medication, and if they received relief, especially with the pain medications.

When you were assigned to patient care, you took care of all of your patients' needs. You might have six patients to care for. This included bed baths, changing the beds, cleaning and dressing wounds, doing colostomy care or tracheotomy care, all the kinds of care I may have mentioned before, plus many more things too numerous to list. There was also complete charting to be done on each patient, including all the care and treatments done and medications given. This was long before the advent of the computer, so it was all done by hand.

I do not remember the exact sequence of my various rotations but want to say a few things about some of them.

During my surgery rotation, we actually scrubbed in, attended, and helped with surgery on any of the cases scheduled for that day. I believe it was a three-month rotation. During this time, I scrubbed or circulated on over 70 different surgeries. That is a lot to see. You also work with a lot of different doctors and staff and get used to taking orders from many different people.

When you scrubbed for surgery, you might be assisting during the operation and hand instruments, help to retract tissue, help to prepare needles and suture, or many other things. You had to know the name of every instrument so when the doctor called for it you could hand it to him quickly and in the proper manner. You also had to be able to set up the instrument tables for each type of surgery with the correct instruments and equipment needed while maintaining strict sterility.

When you scrubbed and circulated, you were able to move about the room. You helped the doctor put on his gown and gloves. You moved about the room taking care of a myriad of jobs that needed to be done during each surgery. You might be required to obtain new sterilized instruments in case one was dropped or was not on the tray and then to hand it to the staff in the correct fashion. You were responsible for counting the sponges at the beginning and the end of surgery to make sure that one was not left in the patient. You might wipe sweat from the brow of the doctor or staff doing the surgery or adjust a headlight. You were available to do whatever needed doing.

We were also on call. This meant that on the day we were scheduled on call we might be called anytime during the evening or night for emergency surgery. You had to go whether you had worked or been in class all day.

I remember well the last night I was on the surgery rotation, and I was on call. I was asleep and got the call around midnight for surgery. When I got there, I changed into scrubs, scrubbed up, and went in. The patient was a middle-aged man shot through the head. The bullet went in through the back of the head, angling from the base of the skull through the head and lodged beneath the skin in the forehead. The patient was first placed on his abdomen and the prep and surgery was set up to start on the back of the head first. Dr. Sugar was the neurosurgeon on call that night. I was one of the scrub nurses assisting during the surgery. I was handing instruments, helping with the suctioning, handing sponges, and doing whatever else was needed. Brain surgery is very slow and tedious. We worked until the day shift came in, and then he was ready to be turned and surgery was started on the front. This was a fascinating way to end my surgery rotation. I never did know if the man survived or not.

Ob-gyn was a fascinating field of nursing. We

spent part of our time in labor and delivery, part in postpartum, and part in the nursery. Each section had its own thrills and challenges. We were studying these in class at the same time. Labor and delivery, of course, was the most fascinating to me—to see the whole process of a woman arriving in labor and to see the babies actually being born. We helped during the whole process. We saw easy births, and then we also saw very difficult births. We saw babies born okay, while others were born deformed, born too early, or even born dead.

Postpartum was also an interesting area. We helped mothers learn to handle their babies, to breast feed, to bathe their babies, and with any other information they required. We also took care of the mother and her related health problems. We took care of C-section surgery patients and all the problems they presented. We taught classes to groups of mothers on how to feed, bathe, dress the infant, and how to hold the baby properly.

I will never forget one assignment I had because of my utmost surprise at the end. I was assigned to care for this woman who was going home that day. It was my job to bring the baby to her room, to dress the baby in its going-home clothes, and to assist mother and baby down to the car. While I was dressing the baby, the husband walked in all dressed up in a suit and tie. It took only a second to realize what the situation was. The husband was a female. That was my first known experience with a gay relationship.

We also spent our time in the nursery caring

for babies, feeding babies, and changing diapers on a whole room full of babies. It was excellent experience, but not an area I would want to work in forever.

We did our psychiatric rotation at a private psychiatric hospital in Chicago. I found psych very interesting. We saw a lot of different psych problems and diagnoses. This was a completely different field of nursing than any other. The medication and treatments were very different.

I had more psych experiences in the later years of my nursing career, when I saw shock therapy used for depression. Ultimately, I became disillusioned with psych doctors and psych methods of treatment. I felt that patients never seemed to really improve and kept returning to the hospital over and over.

We did our pediatric training at Cook County Hospital in Chicago. The experience of working at such a huge hospital was an experience in itself. I remember the halls and rooms full of beds. I saw everything imaginable that could happen to children. I saw abused kids and kids shot or beaten. I saw every kind of deformity you can imagine. One baby I will never forget had a severe cleft palate, and while I was feeding the baby with a bottle, milk came out of the corner of the eye.

The floors were so huge that if you passed medications you never got the medications to the kids on time, and by the time you made one complete round, it was time to start over on the next round.

We worked very hard there. We functioned just

like a regular nurse. I remember being assigned to give all the care, treatments, dressing changes, and everything to this one room. It was a room full of infants and babies that had tracheotomies. That kind of assignment was truly a challenge and frightening for a student and probably even for the regular nurses. We were very challenged the whole time we were there.

We lived in a dormitory there. I had a room of my own at that time. I recall the day that President Kennedy was shot. I was sitting in my room studying when someone came by and told me.

That rotation was during the last year of our training. I was beginning to consider what I wanted to do upon graduation.

As a child and all the time growing up, I dreamed about traveling and seeing the world to learn about other places. I would watch the airplanes fly overhead and know that someday I would be up there too. I knew I would never have the money to travel, so one day I called up the Army Nurse Corp recruiter. She came out and talked to me about joining the Army Nurse Corp. She brought all the paper work with her. Since I was too young to be able to sign for myself, we sent all the forms to Mother to sign and return. I am sure it was a complete surprise to Mother and Daddy, as no one in our family had joined the military yet. I am sure they had legitimate concerns, but they realized this was what I wanted and was a good choice for me. I signed up requesting the chance to be sent to Europe, which is where

I really wanted to travel. Vietnam, at this time, was still not in full swing yet. The Army approved my request for assignment. I was placed on the inactive status where I received $99 a month until I graduated and obtained the results that I had passed the Illinois State Board Nursing Exam. That took about eight months. I would then be in the Army Nurse Corps and up for assignment.

Let me speak to a few more things in general about being in nurses' training at Illinois Masonic Hospital School of Nursing. We started out with 78 students, and two of them were male. I believe our class had the first male students to start training at this school. About two-thirds of us made it to graduation. Some were asked to leave or left for various reasons each year.

As I said, we lived in a dorm and had strict rules to go by. We had curfew and had to be in by a certain time at night. We had a housemother who checked rooms each night. We had uniform inspections. Sometimes we came downstairs in the morning and found faculty sitting at a table to inspect our whole uniform: nylons, shoes, hat, hair, and general appearance. If anything was wrong, we were sent back upstairs to correct it—plus we would be written up. I forget what happened to you after that. We all wore the same kind of uniform. It was a dress-type uniform. Pants were still unheard of then.

Our hospital was located in the northern part of Chicago. It was within walking distance of Wrigley Field, Lincoln Park Zoo, and Lake Michigan.

We also became familiar with riding the city buses to get around or riding the elevated trains. I used to get on the elevated to go to Evanston once in a while to visit June. John also lived in Chicago, and I used to visit him on occasion.

Only a few times, maybe three or four in the time I was gone, I would ride the elevated to the LaSalle Street train station and catch a train to go home for a visit. It went to LaSalle, Illinois, which is about 15 miles from Mother and Daddy. They would come and pick me up there. One time I brought home Jane, a girlfriend from training. That visit was the time mother told me about Rex being gone.

One evening in my freshman year, I was talking to this young lady faculty member in one of the classrooms in the dorm. I am not sure what the reason was, but that was the first time I accepted Christ into my life. As you have noted, we grew up in the church and always went to church, but I had never actually accepted Christ as my Lord and Savior until then.

All in all, nurses training was very hard both academically and work wise. I applied myself completely and must have done it well, because when I took my Illinois State Boards, I passed them with very high scores in all the areas. I had reciprocity that allowed me to work in any state in the United States without having to take the test again. This set me up to be able to work as a nurse and to travel anywhere in the U.S. that I wanted to for the rest of my life.

I worked as an RN for 27 years before I got out of the nursing field and started in a completely new type of work. I will go into more detail about that job later.

I always did an excellent job in whatever area of nursing I chose to work. I always received excellent or exceptional evaluations by my head nurses or by my supervisors for all of my years of work.

Mother was right though; being an RN gave me the ability to take care of myself. I was able to move to various states and to find a job immediately. I will discuss all this in more detail later.

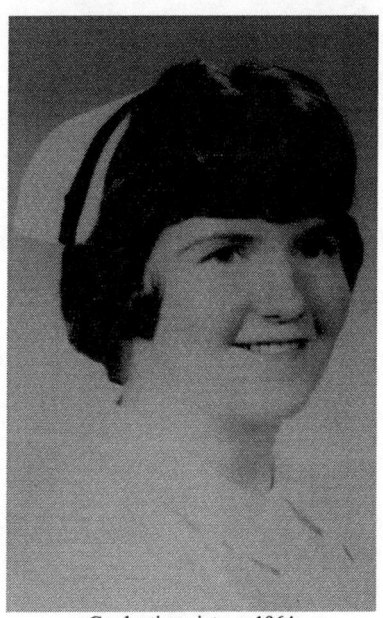

Graduation picture, 1964

Chapter Three - The Army Nurse Corp

BASIC TRAINING — OVERVIEW

After graduation from nurses training on August 7, 1964, I continued to work at the Illinois Masonic Hospital as a grad nurse until I heard from my state boards. Just a side note—the state board exams were very hard and lasted for two days. I took them on August 27–28, 1964. After I finished them, I had no idea whether I had passed or failed so the wait was long.

On October 9, I was working on a ward in the hospital on the day shift. This was on a Friday. It was about 9 a.m. in the morning. They called me out to the desk for a phone call. It was the Army calling. They said that I had passed my boards and was to report to Fort Sam Houston in San Antonio, Texas, by Monday morning. That was less than 2½ days away. I left work immediately and went back to my apartment and packed what little I had and jumped into my car to head south of Chicago a hundred miles to say good-bye to my folks and to pick up a few more things.

When I got home and repacked, Daddy insisted

that I know how to change a flat tire so we went out in the driveway to do just that.

Then I started driving to Texas. I drove very long days, but I did make it in time.

I started a green record book at the beginning of basic training at Fort Sam Houston. I continued writing in this book for part of my first duty station after basic. I have kept this book all of these years and will write it in its entirety a little later in this section.

Starting basic, we were first advised of what clothing items and supplies we would need. I showed a list of about 40 items of clothing and gear, along with the prices, that were needed. I also showed a list of 17 items of clothing and supplies that were issued to us. Part of our first few weeks was spent getting fitted for uniforms, doing paper work, taking care of any medical requirements, and, of course, getting a ton of shots and vaccinations.

I was actually commissioned into the Army Nurse Corp on 19 Oct 64. There were four big buildings around an open field called the Quadrangle. The ceremony was held there. So at that time, I actually became a 2nd Lieutenant. The pay then was $222.00 per month.

I noticed while reading over this record about basic training that there were 3–4 of us girls that had fun and hung out together. We went on dates with the young men there, went dancing, out to eat, to the movies, sightseeing, horseback riding, and even took a helicopter ride. We had fun the whole time we were in basic training. Once we went to Laredo, Mexico. Another time we saw the Alamo and also visited the River Walk in downtown San Antonio.

On Oct. 26, we started the real work. We had formation in the Quadrangle at 7:15 every morning and at 12:15 every afternoon. Our learning to march consisted of drill for 45 minutes every morning, and then we marched to classes. We did a lot of marching while we were there. We even learned parade marching as we had to march in a parade while there. We marched in all kinds of weather, as it was cold and rainy the three months we were there.

Every so often we had rank dress inspection. Your uniform, shoes, hat, and everything had to be just perfect. You stood at attention in formation while inspection was done on each person. It could be long, cold, and miserable at times.

We also started classes this week. They started off with military information such as "Code of Conduct," "The Nurse Corp Song," and "The Nurse's Prayer." We were taught about leadership traits and responsibilities. We learned about mass casualty and burn patients and the parts we were to play as nurses. We had classes in military administration, military science, and nursing classes related to the military. We learned some history about nurses in the military.

We spent some time in the Brooks Army Hospital, working on wards and becoming accustomed to military record keeping and charting. We had classes in basic lifesaving and how to take care of all different types of casualties. I noticed in the record that we even had a class in debriding a high velocity wound on an anesthetized goat. Rather unusual.

On 30 Nov 64, we were getting prepared for our bivouac at Camp Bullis. We lived out there for a few days and set up a field hospital.

A copied excerpt from the record book appears as follows:

Well, we were told some more about the great Camp Bullis today. They had me scared out when they mentioned all the spiders out there. That really bothers me. Some of the other things we can expect to find are snakes, scorpions, rodents, ticks, mites, and other bugs, etc. Plus the weather right now is cold and gets down to freezing. They warned us never to put on our boots without shaking them out real good first to get rid of the spiders, scorpions, etc. We were issued a second duffel bag of equipment. Some of the things in it were a canteen, mess gear, cargo pack, poncho, sleeping bag, 2 blankets, helmet with liner, first aid kit, pistol belt, and a waterproof bag.

The next day we had a four-hour class learning how to use the equipment we had just received—how to fold it correctly for packing and how to care for it. We got everything packed that day, as the next day we would go to Camp Bullis. We got our fatigues and boots and everything ready to wear the next day.

The next morning we got up at three a.m. to get loaded up and ready to go. We arrived at Camp Bullis at 0645. The first day we were taken out in big trucks quite far from camp and taught to read and follow a compass.

We had classes on different ways of transportation, including ambulances in the field, and the 1 & 2 man carry. We had classes on many other things from helicopters to wound care.

One day they took us up on a hill and put on a mock battle below, using fake explosions and smoke. They had jets go over and drop fake bombs. We saw simulated patients carried off the field to field hospitals and then saw how they were handled there.

On 7 Dec 64, we went out again for several days at Camp Bullis. This time we set up tents and all the equipment to run a hospital. We had mock patients to triage and to send on by helicopter or ambulance. We spent time actually working in the mash hospital, as if it was really operating.

Our graduation from basic training was on 18 Dec 64. I left that day for Fitzsimmons General Hospital in Denver, Colorado, which was my next duty station.

The next several pages are my handwritten records, which I kept during basic and during part of my time in Denver. I found the stories fascinating to read, as I had forgotten a lot of stories that were in it. The book brought back many memories. It is presented over approximately the next 100 pages—intact, unedited, and in its entirety.

THE GREEN RECORD BOOK

29 Feb 64
    Inducted into the Army Nurse Corp at Army Recruiting Station on 615 W. Van Buren, Chicago.

7 Aug 64
    Graduated from Illinois Masonic Hospital School of Nursing.

31 Aug 64
    Started work at Masonic Hospital on 3C. I took my state board exams in Chicago on Aug. 27–28, 1964.

26 Sept 64
    I am enjoying my work on 3C. I get standing orders usually. It is real busy but I am learning. I come home every night in anticipation of either a letter from the Army or my state board results. I wish I would know when I leave. Mr. S tells me a lot about it. It sounds fascinating. I do not care much for living in this Melrose apartment. There is too much friction among the four of us (Penny R, Sandra P, Kathy N, and me).

9 Oct 64 Friday
    At a quarter to nine this AM I was working on 3C making a bed when I received my call from the Army to start for Texas. When I found out I

had passed my state boards and was really going now, I shook all over. I don't believe I've ever been so excited before. Everyone was happy but sorry I wasn't staying longer. I packed at the apartment, called mother, Johnny, and Vicki. I couldn't get June and Phil. Then I picked my orders up at 5th Army Headquarters at East Hyde Park. Then I started for home. I got there about 4 PM and packed my car with Roberts help. Dolores, Barb, and Donny came too. I left home at 6 PM. At Bloomington I had to replace two burnt-out headlights which was $5.00. I stopped for the night at 9:30 PM at "Hi Motel Incorp. ($6.00) R.R.2, Stanton, IL. My figures show that from home I covered 162 miles about. I am about 40 miles out of St. Louis. Have to write several postcards to home and to Bonny. I still can hardly believe this is all true. I hope I can make it to San Antonio by Monday.

10 Oct 64 Saturday

This morning I started out at 4 AM. It was good driving because of lack of traffic but it was real cold. I wished for gloves. I had to get a new air filter and 1 can of oil which came to $4.75 altogether. I'm glad the garage men find these things out for me. They are real nice all along the way. I kept passing or seeing this one brown VW all during the morning and finally the driver (a young man) in that car and I were going to meet at a certain place for lunch but somebody got the directions wrong because we never saw each other again. He was heading for Las Vegas, his home. A person sort of gets to know some of the other cars during the day. The truck drivers always wave or toot. In the afternoon this one garage man pointed out that my tires were real bad and showed me all the cuts and knobs in them, so I bought four new tires (almost new) for $100.00. I put it on my credit card so I can pay it later. He also balanced my wheels. I drove 612 miles today. I stopped at 6 PM because I have to set my hair and dry it. My eyes are all bloodshot from so much driving. Have to write a postcard home and tell them about my tires. If I have good driving tomorrow I'll make it to San Antonio on time.

11 Oct 64 Sunday

I started out about 4:30 AM. The motel I stayed at was real nice and cost only $5.10. I drove 485 miles today. I arrived in Fort Sam Houston at 2 PM. The whole trip was 1360 miles from Chicago to San Antonio. F.S.H. is real large and I would guess it is about 5 times the size of Lostant. It has 2 movies, bowling, 2 swimming pools, golf, tennis, stores, and etc. I live in Davidson Hall, a dorm like building. They provide ironing boards, free washers and dryers, and pop and candy machines. My room is nice. I have a large dresser, large desk, real large closet, a big easy chair with a foot stool, an arm chair, a straight chair, 2 desk lamps, a stand lamp, mirror, 2 overnight tables, and of course a bed with an Army blanket. The bathroom is nice with tub and shower. My john mate is a pretty Negro girl by the name of Rachael. We seem to get along just fine and plan to go to classes together. Everyone seems nice here.

12 Oct 64 Monday

Today mainly we had our records checked. Mine haven't arrived yet and I can't be commissioned or receive officer pay until they do. I hope they come soon. The cafeteria or mess hall is real nice. So far the food is good. We eat on tin trays which is different. I had a safety check done on my car by the Texaco station. It is required by the Fort. They had to readjust my headlights. The whole thing cost $3.00. We had a lecture by Major Betz on clothes and supplies we need to get or that are issued to us. There is a whole load of things. On 26 Oct 64 we have our first dress drill and a reception. There is also a riding stable here that costs $4.00 per month plus $1.50 each time you ride for 2 ½ hours. A list of the mandatory purchases is as follows:

1. Cap-wool-Army green---$3.40
2. Skirt-wool-Army green---$5.05
3. Coat-wool-Army green---$20.50
4. Blouse-drip dry-tan---$9.95
5. Necktab-black---$0.35
6. Handbag-leather-black---$15.10

7. Gloves-leather-black---$2.80
8. Skirt-summer green (2)---$8.10
9. Coat-summer green (2)---$15.80
10. Cap-summer green---$15.80
11. Scarf-rayon-tan---$0.40
12. Gloves-cotton-tan---$1.70
13. Sweater-wool-taupe---$6.35
14. Socks-wool-taupe---$1.50
15. Drill shoes---$12.95
16. Dress shoes---$7.00
17. Hat-wool-Army green---$7.15
18. Overcoat-wool-taupe---$36.90
19. Cap-field (baseball type)---$1.10
20. U.S. Army tapes (2)---$0.18
21. Name tapes (6)---$1.12
22. White hose and neutral hose seamless
23. Nameplate----$0.50
24. Raincoat-tan---$4.50
25. Gold band---$1.15
26. White nurses shoes---$12.95
27. 2nd Lt. bars (2)---$1.80
28. Caduceus (2)---$1.90
29. U.S. sets (2)---$1.10
30. Hat insignia---$0.15
31. Army blue dress uniform---$68.60
32. Shirtwaist-white---$9.95
33. Gloves-white---$2.50
34. Shoulder insignia---$6.75 or $12.50
35. Hat-Army blue (field grade)---$40.95
36. Army notebook, pencils, paper, pen, ruler, dividers, etc.

Equipment issued to us as follows:
1. Duffel bag
2. Boots-black (2)
3. Cap-garrison wool
4. Cap-nurse white
5. Cap-field
6. Coat-wind resistant
7. Dress-woman white
8. Gloves-leather
9. Gloves-wool
10. Hood-winter
11. Jacket-woman's wool
12. Liner-coat
13. Shirt-wool
14. Shirt-herringbone
15. Slacks-wool
16. Slacks-sateen
17. Socks

The most important thing I found out today was my first duty station is in Denver, Colorado which was my second choice. I was lucky, most of the kids didn't get their choice and were sent to Kentucky, Georgia, or to the Carolinas.

13 Oct 64 Tuesday

It seems as if you are always hurrying up to wait someplace here. You wait hours sometimes. It all seems very confused in this processing. I went to the quartermaster to be fitted for summer uniforms, etc and boots. I had to go off base and get some black flats which I got 2 for $5.00. I am spending the money like water but will get reimbursed for some of it. I signed up at the "Boots and Saddle" stable to ride while I'm here on base. It was $4.00 a month plus $1.50 each time you ride. I should get riding boots but they are so expensive. They received my papers so maybe tomorrow I will receive my travel check, etc. We had to write an autobiography which I will show here:

Autobiography of Donna Carol Nielsen
21 years of age
"My main reason for joining the Army Nurse Corp is for the traveling opportunities. Also, I believe I will learn many more procedures and ways of nursing than I could in a civilian hospital. Later, I may decide to take advantage of further education offers by the Army. I joined the Army instead of the Navy (she asked this) because the Army offered the Student Nurse Army Program. This financial aid helped me in my senior year of nurses training. I believe the Army will help me to make a better and more mature person.

No member of my immediate family has attended any military training. It was a completely new idea to my family when I told them of my plans to enter this field. They encouraged me and gave me any help they could.

My mother and father are both living and

have three other children besides myself. My older brother is 25 years of age, married, and living near Chicago. My older sister is 23 years of age, married and living in Madison, Wisconsin. My younger brother is 16 and is attending high school.

I graduated from Illinois Masonic Hospital School of Nursing in Chicago, Illinois. My graduation date was 7 Aug 64.

In my freshman year I received the freshman honor award for nursing and personal qualities.

I was on various committees throughout my three years of nurses training.

After graduation, starting 1 Sept 64 I worked on a general medical-surgical floor and enjoyed it. I left this position 9 Oct 64 to come to Fort Sam Houston in Texas." End

14 Oct 64 Wednesday

We were issued our white uniforms and fitted for them. I also found out I had to have part of my physical redone because it was lost so I saw a part of the main hospital. Several of us went bowling on the post lanes. It is a big 24 alley place. In the evening at 8 PM several of us went to the Officer's Club for a dance. They had a band brought in. It was real nice. Early in the evening this medical resident (Harvey) asked me to dance so we danced 3–4 times, and then left to see some of San Antonio. We ended up not seeing too much of it. I don't believe he will ask me out again because we disagreed in one area. He was real nice, 26, Captain, and I enjoyed myself and learned several useful things.

15 Oct 64 Thursday

Today I went to Sugarmans (uniform store downtown) and was fitted for my blue uniform. They also said our 2nd Lt. bars if in good condition at the end of 18 months could just be exchanged for 1st Lt. bars. When my Army financial status was figured out it was noted that I had received too large a check last time, so it will come out of my next checks. That will hurt me some financially. I guess we won't receive any pay till next week so I have to tread lightly.

16 Oct 64 Friday

I went horse back riding for about 2 ½ hours with a group of girls. The major who led us only believes in posting (English style riding) which is very hard to do. I did not much care for it. Rachael found out her 1st duty station is Letterman in San Francisco, Calif. She was real happy. This evening three of us went to a movie downtown (Don't Send Me Flowers). The Majestic Theater was beautiful and large. Their theater was $1.25. Downtown San Antonio, any part, is not to good a section. It isn't safe at all to walk alone or drive with your doors unlocked. San Antonio doesn't seem near as big as Chicago.

17 Oct 64 Saturday
   I and another girl went horseback riding alone and it was a lot nicer. I didn't have to post and got along just fine with western riding.

18 Oct 64 Sunday
   Three of us went to a Calvary Baptist church at 11 AM for church. It is a small church and real nice. The minister delivered a good sermon and I got a lot out of it. In the afternoon four of us went to Breckenridge Park and saw the sunken gardens, a big zoo, etc. It was real pretty. That evening I went to the Union Training class at Calvary. That is the young single people's class. The group seems real nice and accomplishes a lot. After I attended evening worship. Then our group went to a pancake house. I was with a fellow named Charley. We went riding around San Antonio afterward. This fellow was ok but not especially the kind I would pick. He sort of latched on to me. He is enlisted and works in the hospital as a lab technician.

19 Oct 64 Monday
   At 10 AM General McGibony commissioned us. He read and we followed. We were in formation out on the quadrangle. It was real windy and kind of cold. The ceremony only took about 15 minutes. We had TV coverage. After that we went to Blesse Hall to receive a book "The Armed Forces Officer" which we can keep. We

also received our orders plus a big certificate of officer ship. I am now a 2nd Lt.

20 Oct 64 Tuesday

Boy, I thought I had a lot of papers to fill out at school for the Army, but it is nothing like we have here. Today we sat in class for six hours and filled out papers. It was very tiring. Found out we go to Camp Bullis from Nov. 30 to Dec. 9 for field training. That's quite awhile.

21 Oct 64 Wednesday

Today we got pictures and fingerprints taken for new ID cards. We also got our drill shoes downtown at Joskes. They aren't too bad looking and are comfortable. Tonight I and another girl went to the dance at the pit. It was real nice. They always have a good band (five piece usually). It was real crowded. I met this one guy that I remained with all evening. His name was Bob and he is here for a two month course on Hospital Registrar. He is going to take me dining and dancing Friday night at the regular Officer's Club. That is the place we can't go unless we're members or escorted. It should be nice. He told us quite a lot about what to expect in our classes and about drill formation.

22 Oct 64 Thursday

We got our $300.00 uniform allowance today that I have spent already. I have all my uniforms that we have to buy now. We received our booster shots today—tetanus, typhoid, typhus, and smallpox vaccinations. My arm is getting sore and probably will hurt tomorrow. Yesterday we received our books which we will study from in Basic. They are: "Control of Communicable Disease in Man," "Military Sanitation," "Drill and Ceremonies," "Military Leadership," "Psychological Operations," "Preventive Medicine," "Immunizations," "Index of Administrative Publications," and a pamphlet on Medical Service Army Nurse Corps.

We received a "Code of Conduct" card for members of the Armed Forces of the U.S. It is as follows:

1. I am an American fighting man. I serve in the forces which guard my country and our way of life. I am prepared to give my life in their defense.

2. I will never surrender of my own free will. If in command I will never surrender my men while they still have means to resist.

3. If I am captured I will continue to resist by all means available. I will make every effort to escape and aid others to escape. I will accept neither parole nor special favors from the enemy.

4. If I became a prisoner of war, I will keep faith with my fellow prisoners. I will give no information or take part in any action which might be harmful to my comrades. If I am a senior, I will take command. If not, I will obey the lawful

orders of those appointed over me and will back them up in every way.

5. When questioned, should I become a prisoner of war, I am bound to give only name, rank, service number, and date of birth. I will evade answering further questions to the utmost of my ability. I will make no oral or written statements disloyal to my country and its allies or harmful to their cause.

6. I will never forget that I am an American fighting man, responsible for my actions, and dedicated to the principals which made my country free. I will trust in my God and in the United States of America.

This code makes me proud to be an American and in the U.S. Army.

23 Oct 64 Friday

My arm isn't very sore from the shots, it just itches a lot. The smallpox vaccination might take this time. I hope not. Tonight Bob picked me up at 7:00 (right on time). We went to the Officer's Club to eat and had a real good meal. The Club is beautiful, much nicer than the pit. Then he showed me around there. Then he took me to Lackland Air force Base to their Officer's Club. It was real crowded so we didn't stay long because we couldn't find a table. We got back to our Club about 10:30 and danced till one, then went out to eat. I got in around 2:30. It was really nice. I never drank so many cokes in all my life but he accepts the fact very well that I don't drink. He asked me out for Sunday evening.

24 Oct 64 Saturday

I got a wash done on my car at the Standard station. They did a real nice job and also vacuumed the inside. It really needed it. It only cost $1.50. Tonight Rose and Rachael and I went to a drive in movie. It was real good but boy was I tired. They are really two wonderful girls. It is too bad we're going in completely different directions. Rose is going to Walter Reed Hospital in Washington, DC and Rachael is going to Letterman Hospital in San Francisco. Dressing for the first time on Monday for drill really scares me. Mainly because we don't know how to march yet and also we don't know how to salute, and we'll be doing more saluting once we hit that quadrangle. They say that everyone in all four buildings comes out on the balconies to watch our first drill day. Bob say he'll be out there. He also gave me three sets of 2nd Lt. bars which was real nice of him.

25 Oct 64 Sunday

Went to Calvary Baptist Church. Went out with Bob to the Officer's Club for supper and then we danced till around 11:00 and I had to get in a little bit early because of dress drill tomorrow.

26 Oct 64 Monday

Well, we're all very disgusted. It has been beautiful weather up to today when we really wanted it to be nice for dress drill and our reception. But, it is raining real hard and thundering and storming. My raincoat isn't a very good fit because it is too long. I guess I am luckier than some because some couldn't get any at all. Quartermaster was all out. I'm writing this at 06:30 AM so we'll see what I have to say at 6:30 PM about this terrible day. I was scared anyway without all this weather to top if off.

Well, tonight I can truthfully say today was really bad. When we went out it was really raining hard and our shoes got soaked before we got to the car. Instead of having us march to our classroom (theater) as we were supposed to they just had us go as we were. Water covered half the streets on either side and lay in the grass like swamp land. We really got bedraggled looking even though some of us had raincoats. My hair looked like something from another planet as did some others. We have to march to classes and we have formation at 07:15 AM and 12:15 PM. Marching is rather hard so far. It is hard to keep in step, dress right, (in line) and keep up their pace. I think I look ok in uniform except the cap smashes my hairdo on the top pretty bad. We are really in the swing of classes now. It is not going to be easy. We have a lot to learn and only a short time to do it in. They grade on a point system. The total is 1000 points. (All on exams).

Exams

Two week comprehensive	100 pts.
Dept. Military Science	125 pts.
Dept. of Administration	125 pts.
Dept. of Nursing (Preventive Med) (Vet. Science) (Neuro-Psych) (Med-Surg and Dental) (Nuclear Science)	400 pts.
Practical exercises, field exercises, Hospital experiences and Personal qualities	250 pts.
Total	1000 pts.

The grades are:
A—-superior 92–100
B—-Very satisfactory 86–91
C—-Satisfactory 77–85
D—-Borderline 70–76
U—-Unsatisfactory 60–69

If you do not get 70 or over you would retake basic training. We were told we have the holidays of Nov. 11, 26, and 27 off. We will have 4 days in the field at Camp Bullis and 3–4 days in the Brooks General Hospital.

27 Oct 64 Tuesday
We are really learning how to drill. I guess we

will have about 14 hours instruction in it. We saw a parade today that was very impressive. Today we received our "Honorable Discharge" from the Army of the United States as a PFC (E 3) WAC USAR. It is real nice which I will send home when possible to keep. I received a letter from home today giving me my state board results. I was real pleased because I got national reciprocity.

My results are as follows: The Illinois low score is 350.
Surg. 591—Med. 531—OB 513—Peds. 575—Psych 562.

We received some info in class that I would like to have a record of:

Principals of Field Medical Service
There are 12 principals but the over all objective is "To conserve the fighting strength."
1. Continuity—Uninterrupted medical support. "Lag time" before treatment not over 6 hours. Treat during evacuation.
2. Proximity—Bring patient and treatment facility close together. Keep forward facilities cleared of patients. Keep medical means as far forward as the battle permits.
3. Control—Medical service must control both patient and med means. Control should be centralized as far as possible. Decentralized control

usual in rapid or independent or retrograde operations.

4. Simplicity—Of med tactics, of treatment procedures. More complexity possible at rear installations. Avoid immobilizing forward medical facilities.
5. Flexibility—Maintain a reserve of means—not of people. Have alternate plans.
6. Mobility—Prerequisite to flexibility. Must match mobility of supported troops. Impossible without prompt clearing of forward facilities.
7. Conformity—To accepted professional practice and highest med standards. To the tactical situation and to the realities of the climate, terrain, and enemy capabilities. Med service must be unobtrusive at right time, in right place, and in right amount.
8. Distribution—Place med people and means to favor areas of greatest casualty density. Require accurate information of current operations, future plans.
9. Supporting Levels Provide Evacuation—Zone of med responsibility is toward the front. Evacuation means are sent forward to pick up patients then return to point of origin.
10. Sorting—"Triage" The decision who will be returned directly to duty, who held for treatment here, who promptly evacuated. Requires greatest med judgment, skill and experience. Done at every level of evacuation line. Effectives must be retained.

11. Mission—Each facility at each level has specific, designed capability. Each must work to the limit of its capability but not exceed it. Assure uniform quality of med care.
12. Greatest Service to Greatest Numbers—Definitive treatment often not possible far forward. Medical means never unlimited. Means must be used economically to ensure maximum numbers receive care.

On the following page, I would like to portray "Hospitalization Evacuation Systems, Theater of War."

On the two pages after that, I would like to portray the different ranks and insignia in the Army for the enlisted, warrant officer, and commissioned.

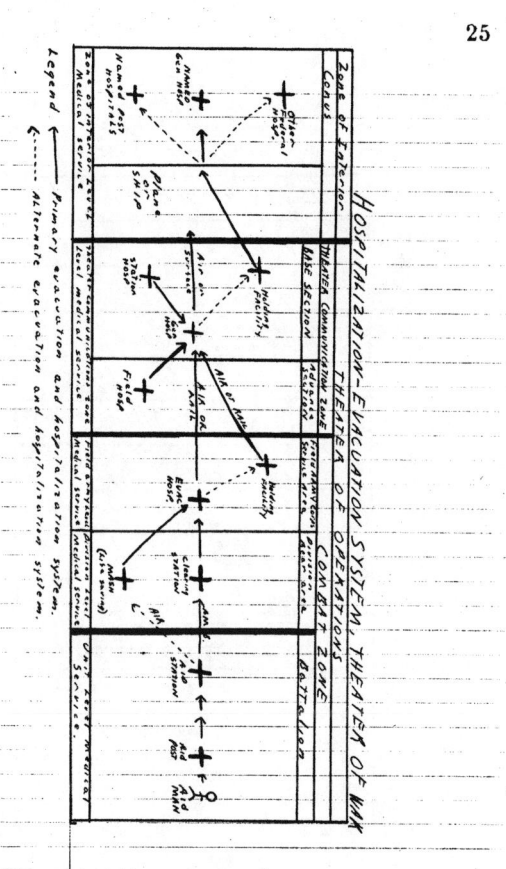

I would like to portray the different ranks and insignia in the army.

	ENLISTED			
E1	No insignia	PRIVATE		
E2	No insignia	PRIVATE		
E3	∧	Private First Class		
E4	∧∧	CORPORAL	3rd	SPECIALIST FOUR
E5	∧∧∧	SARGEANT	3rd	SPECIALIST FIVE
E6		STAFF SARGEANT	3rd	Specialist SIX
E7		Platoon Sarg. or Sarg First Class	3rd	Specialist Seven
E8		MASTER or FIRST SARGEANT		
E9		Sargeant MAJOR		

	WARRANT OFF.		
W1	[Brown/Gold bar]	WARRANT Grade One	
W2	[Brown/Gold bar]	WARRANT Grade Two	
W3	[Brown/Silver bar]	WARRANT Grade Three	
W4	[Brown/Silver bar]	WARRANT Grade Four	

29

COMMISSIONED			
01	▭ Gold	Second Lieutenant	
02	▭ Silver	First Lieutenant	COMPANY OFFICER
03	▭▭ Silver	Captain	
04	🍂 Gold oak leaf	Major	FIELD
05	🍂 Silver oak leaf	Lieutenant Colonel	OFFICER
06	Eagle	Colonel	
07	☆ star	Brigadier General	
08	☆☆	Major General	GENERAL
09	☆☆☆	Lieutenant General	OFFICER
010	☆☆☆☆	General	
011	☆☆☆☆☆	General of the Army	

CAP INSIGNIA

OFFICER - EAGLE.

WARRANT - EAGle & wreath.

Enlisted - EAGle in circle.

28 Oct 64 Wednesday

We are really learning a lot in drill but it is rather hard. We drill 45 minutes every morning, then to classes. We received our flu shots today. We also had the TB (tine) test. I had my hair cut at the post beauty shop. I hope it works out ok. Our green wool hats we wear really mash it. Thank goodness we leave them on except for class. I received mail from home including my nurse's registration wallet card, my RN certificate, my state board grades, and my motor club info wallet card and car stickers. I think our uniforms look pretty sharp. I can't wait to get done with basic. Right now we have classes all day and it is really confusing, especially about organization of the Army and Army Medical Corps. We have a lot to learn in a short time.

29 Oct 64 Thursday

We learned several new steps or procedures in marching. We received shots for yellow fever. This evening we practice marching (those who want to) in our parking lot for an hour and a half. I am very tired and my feet ache tonight.

Army Nurse Corps Song
Music—Lou Singer
Words—Pvt. Hy Zaret

*"We march along with faith undaunted,
Beside our gallant fighting man,*

*Whenever they are sick or wounded,
We nurse them back to health again.
As long as healing hands are wanted,
You'll find the nurses of the corps.
On ship or plane or transport train,
At home or on a far-off shore,
With loyal hearts we do our part,
For the Army and the Army Nurse Corps."*

The Nurse's Prayer
**Words and Music—Edith A Aymes,
Maj. ANC retired**

"Father, the soldier seems so close to you, please let me not forget what he's been through, His tired face is dark with pain. Lend him your strength till he smiles again. Help me to keep him safe, lest I should fail, that pledge I gave to Florence Nightengale. If he must go, then I will know, you called him home, cause you loved him so. While angels watch and guard his rest. Help me to know I have done my best."

30 Oct 64 Friday

This evening Rose and I went to the pit for dancing. Harvey was there and we danced for half an hour and he found out I had still not changed my mind on our previous disagreement. After that Bob came in and I spent the rest of the evening with him. He asked me out to the Officer's Club for dinner and dancing Sunday night. We have a lot of fun. Rose met a friend of Bobs called Vick. He seemed real nice. He is from Puerto Rico.

I would like to portray a list of Leadership Traits as follows:
1. Knowledge—Acquired info including professional knowledge and an understanding of your subordinates.
2. Courage (Physical and Moral)—A mental quality which recognizes fears of danger or criticism but enables the individual to meet dangers or opposition with calmness and firmness.
3. Initiative—A quality of seeing what has to be done and commencing a course of action.
4. Decisiveness—Ability to make decisions promptly and then express them in a clear and forceful manner.
5. Tact—The ability to deal with others without creating offense. Need 100%.
6. Justice—Being impartial and consistent in exercising command.
7. Dependability—The certainty of proper performance of duty.
8. Bearing—Creating a favorable impression in carriage, appearance, and personal conduct at all times.
9. Endurance—Mental and physical stamina measured by the ability to stand pain, fatigue, distress, and hardship.

10. Enthusiasm—The display of sincere interest and exuberance in the performance of duties.
11. Unselfishness—The avoidance of providing for ones own comfort and personal advancement at the expense of others.
12. Integrity—Uprightness of character and soundness or moral principle, the quality of absolute truthfulness and honesty.
13. Loyalty—Faithfulness to country, the Army, your unit, your senior, and subordinates.
14. Judgment—Weighing facts and possible solution on which to base sound decision.

Leadership Principles

1. Be technically and tactically proficient.
2. Know yourself and seek self improvement
3. Know your men and look out for their welfare.
4. Keep your men informed.
5. Set the example.
6. Insure the task is understood, supervised and accomplished.
7. Train your men as a team.
8. Make sound and timely decisions.
9. Develop a sense of responsibility among subordinates.
10. Employ your command in accordance with its capabilities.
11. Seek responsibility and take responsibility for your actions.

31 Oct 64 Saturday

We had to get a dental check this morning. I was lucky again. I did not have any cavities. I haven't had any work done in four years. Another girl and I went out on blind dates this evening. We went to the post movie. After I got in I found out I had seen it already. I didn't care for my date too much. He was conceited. He was an MSC. We went on a double date.

1 Nov 64 Sunday

Went to Calvary Baptist Church with Rose today. I settled down and studied some of my military service notes this afternoon. Bob and I went out to Lackland Air force Base this evening for supper at 6:30. It was real good. Then we went into the main club room. There was hardly anyone there all night so it was real quiet. We talked until 1:00. I learned a lot about him. He has had 4 years in the seminary which he studied for the priesthood. He dropped out of this and took 4 years of college so he has been studying most of his life. He did work in a bank when he was a civilian. When he is out he'll either do that or work as a hospital registrar which he will be qualified for through courses taken here in the Army. He is real nice and we have no problems talking with each other. It is too bad he is only going to be here three more weeks. He is a lot of fun.

2 Nov 64 Monday
   Classes are quite hard. We have rather long hours here having to be up at 5:30 AM and usually not getting back here till around 6:00 PM. I am starting to study more now. There is so much to learn. We have to stand at attention for the teacher at the beginning of each class. It seems so odd to do even yet.

3 Nov 64 Tuesday
   Our drill instructor said we marched pretty well today. At noon we had a class picture taken on the bleachers in the quadrangle. I hope it comes out well. I ordered one for two dollars.

4 Nov 64 Wednesday
   I just got up and noted that it is raining out. It is going to be another messy day I guess. I got my duffel bag today. Well, it rained all day long. They held up the morning drill to see if it would stop. As you can guess, it didn't. So at 3:15 PM we went out in the rain with all the puddles on the quadrangle and marched for an hour. Our shoes got thoroughly soaked and we were generally uncomfortable. They were teaching us how to march in a parade as they say we are going to have to do.

5 Nov 64 Thursday
   When I got to my car this evening the motor was completely dead. It wouldn't even make a

sound. I discovered I had left my lights partially on all day. So I went to the MP's and they used their car and my jumpers and got it started. I had it checked out at a gas station to see if the battery was ok. Thank goodness it was.

General Duty Nurse
MOS Code 3449

Summary: Performs basic professional nursing duties in care and treatment of various types of patients of a medical treatment facility.

Duties: Assists in planning, supervising, and rendering daily nursing care of patients. Rotates among the various nursing service activities of the facility, such as general medical, surgical, psych, OB, operating room, anesthesia, and preventive medicine. Supervises and directs ancillary nursing personnel in care and treatment of patients on the ward or in the clinic. Exercises judgment in determining when care required demands the attention of the professional nurse or when it can adequately be given by ancillary nursing personnel. Observes, recognizes, and records symptoms and conditions of patients, calling attention of the head nurse or physician to matters having bearing on recovery of the patient. Assists physicians in therapeutic procedures and administers prescribed medication and treatments in accordance with approved nursing techniques. Assists in evaluation of the performance of nursing service personnel and standards of nursing care in the ward or in the clinic. Assists in maintaining an environment that is conducive to the physical, social, and psychological well being of the patients, families, and duty personnel.

6 Nov 64 Friday

This evening Rose, Rachael and I went for a steak dinner at the Pit. After we stayed for dancing. I met a Veterinarian named George early in the evening. A little later Bob came so I was with him all evening. About 11 PM we went to the Officer's Club to the Ravenroom and danced, and then we went out to eat. I didn't get in till 2:30 AM and had to get up at 5:30 for formation and class in the morning. I didn't end up with much sleep. Bob is real nice. I always have a good time when I go out with him. To bad he leaves in two weeks.

7 Nov 64 Saturday

Today, out on the parade ground every MP (military police) was out, on and around the area. A bus load was off to one side. They had the fire engine and ambulance out by the helicopter landing area. They made all of us go to our rooms and we could not be outside. They checked all the cars in the parking lot to see if they belonged there. They even had four MPs on the roof of

Davidson Hall. We asked one of them what was going on and he said "Top Secret." So we watched out the windows because we thought somebody important was being brought in to the hospital. But after awhile everyone left. It was just a maneuver for the MPs. That was disappointing for us.

8 Nov 64 Sunday

We didn't go to church today, one reason was I had to catch up on lost sleep and also I have to study all day for our test on Monday. There is a lot to study for.

Last week in class they gave us a lecture telling what is expected a nurse should know and do in a mass casualty situation.

I will list as follows:
1. Assist in major or minor surgery.
2. Operate a casualty sorting station.
3. Administration and collection of blood.
4. Burn patient management to include IV therapy.
5. Use and aftercare of tubes.
6. Special nursing procedures.
7. Complete pre and post operation care.
8. Airway management including surgery.
9. Simple anesthesia.
10. Suturing techniques.
11. Psychological care.
12. Circulating and scrub nurse duties.

13. Preparation of sterile supplies.
14. Plus all first aid measures, dressing all wounds, stop bleeding, treat and prevent shock, evacuation and transportation of patients, plus organization of people to help care for the patients.

 We are expected to do a great deal. Right now I feel unconfident. I hope I learn all I need to know here. The lectures we are receiving are very good.
 We received the Brooke Formula for the burn patient which I am not listing here. Also we learned about the three depths of a burn.

1. 1st degree—partial thickness of epidermis is red. No fluid loss or break in the skin.
2. 2nd degree—complete epidermis except real deep layers of it. Red, blisters, heals from the bottom. Does not need a skin graft.
3. 3rd degree—all skin layers and maybe muscle and deep structures involved. Heal only with a skin graft. Is pearl white or charred in color.

9 Nov 64 Monday
 Last night Rose and I went to the post theater and saw "The Moonspinners." It was good. I was surprised by one thing. At the beginning of all military movies they play the "Star Spangled Banner." If you are in civilian clothes you stand at attention, if in your uniform you salute. Another thing, when they raise and lower the flag on the post in the morning and evening—if

you are outside or if you are driving you have to stop, get out of your car and salute as it is lowered.

10 Nov 64 Tuesday
This evening I went out with Bob to a movie downtown. We had a real nice time. We stopped afterward for a coke. We also saw the river that runs through San Antonio. It is real nice to walk beside and very pretty.

11 Nov 64 Wednesday
Rose, Rachael and I went to San Marcus today—about 50–60 miles from here. We saw the Wonder Cave. It was ok but not too long. We also went in a house with no gravity, or so it said. Everyone stood crooked, things would roll up hill, water would go up hill, and a broom stood up by itself. Then we saw the aquarena show with the two swimming ladies and a clown. It was very interesting. We saw an old western village with a lot of ancient equipment, an old saloon, a blacksmith, and etc.

12 Nov 64 Thursday
It rained a little bit today, of all things. I tried on my field clothes from the duffel bag. They are rather funny looking. Tonight a lady from Avon came on my call and I bought a few products. Rose and Rachael have fixed me up with a date to go to Mexico on Thanksgiving. It should be

fun. We are triple dating. To bad Bob is gone before this. I'd rather go with him. We'll see??

13 Nov 64 Friday

Today was our last real day of drill. Is that ever nice. We will have a rank dress inspection next Tuesday though it scares us all. I saw both Harvey and Bob several times today. Harvey talked to me for about half an hour at Happy Hour in the Pit. He knows I haven't changed my mind. I got an 88—B on my Comprehensive Test. A group of us also saw our counselor Major Sheridan for the first time. After this it is individual counseling. We (Rose and I) are going to the dance at the Pit tonight. I hope we have a good time. The dance was nice. After we were there about an hour Bob took Rose and I over to the Ravenroom. It was the first time Rose had seen it. She met some guy there and he took her home. Bob and I went for a long drive. Well, he has only one more week now before he returns to Fort Ritchie, Maryland. I probably won't get to see him again. It was real nice knowing him for these last four weeks. We had a lot of fun.

14 Nov 64 Saturday

I went to the USAA building and took out military auto insurance. They are at a much lower rate than Axlines. This evening Rose and I were driving (I was driving) on highway 35 about 40–50 miles out of San Antonio. I was going the speed limit of 60 when, as this other car passed, something hurled into my window right in front of me. All of a sudden it seemed like a loud explosion and I was hit with glass all over me. My face felt like it had pricks all over it and any other exposed skin did too. I kept control of the car and slowed down and pulled off the side of the road and stopped. That was the first time I could actually see what happened. Right in front of me was a very mashed indentation the size of a soft ball and the whole glass on my side was pretty well smashed with a number of cracks running to the other side. The dashboard and seat were covered with glass including us and our clothes. It even flew back to the back window ledge and in the backseat. The first thing I did was take my flashlight and check my face to make sure I wasn't all cut up. Thank goodness it was ok. By that time I was very angry, confused, and worried—hoping my insurance covered this and wondering why this had to happen. We got out and shook the bigger pieces off and scraped the bigger pieces off the seat so we could sit. My arms were covered with fine layers of glass that felt like grit. I only got a couple of small scratches on them. Rose was ok. I drove back (sitting to one side to see) to San Antonio and stopped at the Standard station where they vacuum cars and did the whole inside. I'll probably still find glass for a month. They told me that a bottle had been thrown at it. Probably it was a whisky or beer bottle. It must have been full to do the damage it did. Nothing like that ever happened to me before and it really startled us. First thing I thought was that it was a bullet. All the way back I kept crunching glass in my mouth and taking minute pieces out of my eyes. Called home too.

15 Nov 64 Sunday

After church Rose and I went to the Headquarters of the 4th U.S. Army. It was originally the first permanent military post established in San Antonio. W.W. Belknap made this effort when he served as Secretary of War under President Ulysses S. Grant. It was begun in 1876 and cost $90,000. It was completed in 1879. In 1886 this fort captured Geronimo and a small band he led. There were deer, peacocks, duck and several other kinds of birds running around loose on the inside. You could walk up and pet them. It is the first time I have ever seen an Albino deer.

16 Nov 64 Monday

Sometimes on our way to school we pick up any guys at the bus stop outside their dorm and give them a ride to school. Several times we've happened to give this Colonel from Thailand a ride. Well, today he was there so we gave him a ride and he invited all four of us (Rose, Rachael, Barbara and I) out for a Chinese dinner on Friday evening at six. We accepted. It should be fun and also we're a little flattered that a person of his rank asked us. I had my first individual counseling with Major Sheridan today. She told me some about Denver and about overseas. I also received a folder on Denver and Fitzsimmons from the CO there. It was very informative. I took my car to "Tom Bensons" today to get a new glass put in. I had to leave it overnight. I hope there is no problem with my insurance. I saw Bob shortly at supper time. I'm going to miss going out with him after he leaves Friday. Tomorrow we have rank dress inspection. I've polished all my brass and pressed my uniform, polished my shoes, did my hair and anything else I could think of. I hope I pass ok.

17 Nov 64 Tuesday

Well, today our company got in formation and all prepared for rank dress inspection and it started to rain so it is postponed till Thursday. So I'll have to get ready for it all over again. I picked up my car today and the insurance covered it ok. They did a good job so it appears. I sent my insurance papers from Axlines home to be cancelled. I am studying for the test on Thursday in Administration. I thought I'd insert a few notes on our formation and marching. Our whole class is split into two groups called companies. My company has about 77 kids in it. Each company is split up into two groups called platoons. Each platoon consists of four lines called squads. I am in the second platoon and second squad. A few of the marching steps we are taught are as follows: right face, left face, about face, rear march, left flank, right flank, left column, right column, left and right oblique, change time, mark time, and a few others. We are also learning to march in parade formation. That means we march with a large group using ten across instead of just four. It makes marching a little different and I feel a little easier. When you begin marching at the command of "forward march" you always start off on your left foot. On some days the MFSS band is out on the quadrangle and we march to music. Sometimes that seems a little harder than just counting cadence. Your left foot hits every time the drum beats.

18 Nov 64 Wednesday

I received my maps and route today from the Chicago Motor Club. I also got my class picture today. Tonight about 9 PM Bob called and asked me to meet him at the Pit. Said to bring Rose too because he had a friend there. Said he wanted to say goodbye to me and Rose because this would probably be the last time we saw him. I was so happy he called. We got there around 9:30 and danced awhile at the Pit, then went to the Raven-room till midnight and danced. We had a lot of fun. Then Bob and I went for a drive where we almost had an accident. He kissed me while he was driving and must not have watched the road.

When he looked up we were heading straight for a sign. He quickly swung the wheel and as a result we skidded around a complete circle till we were turned the other way. Luckily it was late enough that no cars were around. Well, so this is goodbye to Bob. I probably won't ever see him again. I may hear some about him from Rose in Walter Reed because he is going to show Rose around Washington. I think that is really nice of him.

19 Nov 64 Thursday

We had our Administration exam today. I didn't think it was too bad, but I better wait and see before I say too much. This afternoon at 3:30 PM we had our rank dress inspection with Major Betz. The weather was around 45–50 degrees and it was real windy and real cold. We couldn't wear anything except our green cord uniform so we stood there and shivered for 45 minutes. It is hard enough to stand in one place that long without hardly moving and not moving at all when you are at attention. She didn't find anything wrong with my uniform which made me glad. Then right after that, still in that awful cold weather, we practiced for an hour and a half on parade marching because we put on a formal parade next Tuesday. I didn't see Bob at all today because he had had a dinner engagement with this chaplain friend of his that was planned quite some time ago. Bob leaves tomorrow morning.

This evening was our class (ANC) party, and it was a hootenanny. Rose and Rachael and I went for awhile, and then Rose and I went to the Post Theater and saw "Unsinkable Molly Brown." It was good.

20 Nov 64 Friday

Bob left today. Rose, Rachael and I went out to a Chinese dinner this evening at 6 PM with Colonel Yang and two of his friends. They are from Thailand. Colonel Yang's real name is Colonel Yang Vijragupta, MD, MPH. He is in the Army Medical Department of the Royal Thai Army. For the past six years he has been Commander of a hospital over in Thailand. He is also a V.I.P. and is treated as such wherever he goes. I think this is fascinating that we were asked out by him. One of the other fellows name was Captain Anouchit Kanchanagom, MC of the Royal Thai Army. The other fellow was a Lieutenant of the Royal Thai Army but I do not have the correct name. They took us to a Chinese Inn for dinner and there were about six different Chinese dishes. They were quite different tasting than American food and I did not especially like it but it was a good experience. We also attempted to use chopsticks. That was a laugh. We topped off the meal with a good old American Coke!! Then they asked us to go to a movie downtown which we did. We saw the "Young Lovers." It was pretty good. We found out quite a bit about their Army and country. The country is about the size of Texas. The Army consists of 20,000 people including dependants. He wants to take us out again next Wednesday for dinner. We'll let him know Monday. He also wanted to take us out December 17, the day before we leave. He said if he was in Denver before he left he would stop and see me. All three of us girls felt very privileged that he asked us. At the Chinese Inn, he also introduced us to a man there that is a Prince of Laos. After we got back from this date we went to the Pit for part of the dancing for a short while.

21 Nov 64 Saturday
Rose and I, while out on a drive, came across the road to Camp Bullis so we drove down. It is real hilly and bushy country. It is really out in the open spaces but covered with trees, bushes, rocks, etc. It should be real interesting to be out there four days. I picked up my Army green wool today. It fits pretty nice. I'm going to have to catch up on some sleep. I am getting bushed. I called Bonnie.

22 Nov 64 Sunday
Nothing too much happened today. Rose and I went to the downtown theater.

23 Nov 64 Monday
I went out with Harvey tonight. For some reason

I like him. He knows I still haven't changed my mind about anything. I probably won't go out with him again. I usually end up very confused about everything. Anyway, in a week and a half he transfers to the Panama Canal Zone.

24 Nov 64 Tuesday

At 6:30 AM was the Thanksgiving breakfast at the Kooney room in the Pit. All the big heads of MFSS were there and after different speeches were given then a sextet made up of ANC officers sang. At 7:30 AM was the big parade. We were allowed to wear our raincoats because it has been pretty cold lately down here. Our ANC Company led the parade. We had to stand on the quadrangle for about ½ hour while all the citations and awards were given. Boy you get sore all over standing like that for so long. Everybody said we looked good but we have done better in practice.

25 Nov 64 Wednesday

We had our Military Science exam today and boy, it wasn't easy. I don't know how I did. I got results from my Administration exam. I got 121 points out of 125, so that was good. This afternoon I called the Helicopter Port to inquire about getting a ride for Rose, Rachael, Barbara, and myself. So we went out at 4:30 PM and got a half hour ride. That is the most fascinating thing I have ever done. I really enjoyed it. Everything looks so tiny and neat from above. We went up 2000 feet and went about 120 miles an hour. I hope I can ride again sometime.

26 Nov 64 Thursday

Thanksgiving—Rose, Rachael, I, and two guys went to Laredo, Mexico today. We started out about 7:30 AM and it is 150 miles. We got down to Laredo around 10:30. We left the car parked on the U.S. side and walked across the bridge over the Rio Grande to Mexico. The streets are lined with shops packed full of things like leather goods, jewelry, glassware, blankets, clothes, etc. They all try and really sell their goods. They start off with some high price and you act as if you are not interested and they keep lowering it. The things they sell are very good and worth the price. I felt odd about asking for a lower price. We were told before we went it was best not to eat or drink anything over in Mexico except Coke or pop so that is what we did. I didn't buy anything but I did get some Mexican money for my coin collection. I got 3 bills—2 five peso bills and 1 20 peso bill. In coins I got 4 silver pesos, and 4 centavos. A peso is worth 8 cents in American money. We left Mexico around 4 PM and decided to go to Laredo Air force Base on the American side for our Thanksgiving dinner but they were closed when we got there. So we went to a Holiday Inn. We got back to FSH, Texas about 9 PM. It was a real enjoyable day.

27 Nov 64 Friday

Rose, Rachael and I went to a drive in movie this evening. We saw "The Prize" and "Your Cheating Heart" which was the life story of Hank Williams, the western folk singer. Both were good.

29 Nov 64 Sunday

Rose and I went to church this morning. It is really a wonderful church with always a good message. After dinner Rose and I went to the Alamo. It was quite interesting. It listed all of the men that fought and died there, had pictures of some, had displays of guns, money, cannon balls, parchments, etc. Then I showed Rose the underground river of San Antonio. I had seen it before with Bob but enjoyed seeing it again.

30 Nov 64 Monday

Well, we were told some more about the great Camp Bullis today. They had me scared out when they mentioned all the spiders out there. That really bothers me. Some of the other things we can expect to find are snakes, scorpions, rodents, ticks, mites, and other bugs. Plus the weather right now is quite cold and gets down to freezing. They warned us never to put our boots on without shaking them out real good first to get rid of the bugs. We were issued a second duffel bag of equipment. Some of the things in it were a canteen, mess gear, cargo pack, poncho, sleeping bag, 2 blankets, helmet with liner, first aid kit, pistol belt, and a water proof bag. I can say one thing. It was mighty heavy. One of our classes today was a tour. We saw different kinds of latrines, showers, waste disposal units, etc. It was quite interesting but I hope I'm never in the position to use them. I got my dress blues today. They fit pretty well and look real sharp. I got my pay check today and I spent most of it on my car, book payments, for USAA insurance and tire payments. I answered the letter I received from my Chief of Nursing Service at my next duty assignment. The other girl riding with me to Fitzsimmons will pay half of the gas expense there. It should be a three day trip I expect.

1 Dec 64 Tuesday

Today we had four hours in class of just learning how to wear the field clothing and pack our duffel bags. We had to learn how to roll the sleeping bags, blankets, air mattress, and poncho. It has to be done a certain way. We learned how to care for our mess kit which consists of a two piece tin tray with a handle, knife, spoon, fork, and a big tin cup. We learned how to set up our pistol belt. In the back center we put our rolled poncho. On the right front over the hip area is our canteen in its case. The cargo pack that we carry in our hand is the size of a bowling bag and in it are the mess kit and any personal items we need. This evening we got all of our field clothes ready to go and packed our duffel bags and cargo bags. I think mine is all ready now. It sure isn't any fashion show. They said the weight of the field uniform with boots and belt (loaded) is 12 pounds alone. They are going to start loading the truck with our duffel bags at 4:15 tomorrow morning. We leave the post here at 5:45 and are to arrive at Camp Bullis at 7 AM.

2 Dec 64 Wednesday

We got up at 3AM, packed our duffel bags into the truck at 4:15 and loaded the bus to go to breakfast at the mess hall at 5 AM. We left FSH at 5:45 and reached Camp Bullis at 6:45 AM. The first thing we had was an hour class explaining waste disposal, sanitation, etc. Then we loaded onto the trucks (a bench on each side). It was covered with canvas and the back was open. We were taken to an area quite far from camp to do map and compass reading. We were divided into groups with four in each group. We were given certain numbers (azimuths) that we were to follow on the compass until we came to a pre-destined sign. Then we had another number to follow from that sign. One member of the group read the compass and lined it up on another member some distance ahead and then we proceeded to that point and then repeated the process. The whole thing took three hours. The terrain was all hills and valleys. It was covered with brush, a lot of trees, stickier clumps of grass and deadwood. It was also very rocky. It was sometimes quite hard for the person reading the compass to site through a bunch of trees and shrubbery which was often quite thick. It wasn't so cold today so we had on T-shirt, fatigues, black wool socks, black calf length boots, belt, field jacket, and the helmet with the liner. Boy the helmet really flattens the hair. At noon we ate for the first time in our mess kits. You go through the mess line and then you go to tents with tables standing chest high. You eat standing up which is quite novel. In the afternoon we had classes, one explaining and demonstrating the different transportation ambulances and ways to do 1–2 man patient carry. We also had classes demonstrating uses of 3 different types of helicopters for patient transportation. Our last class was demonstrating the different degrees or severity of wounds due to high and low velocity weapons. At 5:30 we had our standing up supper. In the evening we had a half hour film on the life of a basic Army nurse mainly at FSH. It was a recruiting film that is rather new yet.

3 Dec 64 Thursday

Boy, am I bushed today. This is really a lot of physical exercise plus being loaded down with heavy clothes and belt, etc all of the time. This morning we had classes on care given to wounds in each area of the body at the battalion unit level and the clearing station level. In the afternoon they took the whole class way up on top of this hill and we sat on bleachers. We could see all the countryside below us. Then they put on a mock battle for us using fake explosions that made a real loud sound and a cloud of white smoke. They had a jet go over and supposedly drop fake bombs. They had the first aid man checking patients on the field and giving first aid. The litter bearers carried the patients off and the field ambulances and helicopters took them away. It was very realistic. Then we saw how patients were cared for in the different hospitals along the route of evacuation. We left Camp Bullis at 6 PM and got back here around 7 PM. Boy did we feel dirty and tired and beat. Well, so ends our 1st 2 days at Camp Bullis. We go back next Monday and Tuesday.

I would like to describe a few individual items of interest. After we eat, we scraped our mess kits, and then we had to wash them. To accommodate for the large numbers you have in the Army you first wash them with a brush in can 1 which is hot soapy water, then in can 2 which is hot water, and then in can 3 which is a rolling boil. Then you air dry. The mess kit has two parts. When open part 2 sits on the handle of part 1. You have to hold it in the middle to support it. When washing you attach all the silverware and the tin cup to the mess kit and then hold the handle to dunk it in the three cans. When dry you put the silverware in the part 1 side and then put part 2 side over the handle on top of part one and lock the handle in place over all. If we have to carry them with us in the field we put them inside our jacket. Your cup is the same shape as the canteen so it fits on the outside of the canteen with both in the jacket. The barracks we lived in at Camp Bullis were quite different. It was one building with about 4–5 big rooms for the 120 some girls. Each room had a lot of beds in it. They weren't really beds. They were a canvas cover stretched on legs. We used sleeping bags on top to sleep in.

4 Dec 64 Friday

This was my first day in the hospital. I was in Beach Pavilion, 42—G floor. It was an EENT floor. We spent most of the day in conference with the head nurse. She went over the use of charts, her floor, and etc. She also was the only head nurse to give any students an assignment. Each girl on her floor (4 of us) has to give an in-service program. Each one has to make out the whole duty roster for all the personnel on the floor. Each one has to turn in a suggestion on how the floor could be improved. The first two assignments are hard especially. I think, (if I can find enough material) I will do my in-service program on the eye, some disorders of, some surgery, and of the nursing care. The in-service program is given to all of the personnel on the ward, officer and enlisted alike. I hope I do ok. This evening Rose and I went out to supper with

Colonel Yang. It was a Chinese supper and I liked it better than the last one. He also promised to give me some coins from Thailand next week. I think that is real considerate.

5 Dec 64 Saturday

Boy!! I really splurged today. I went shopping at Joske's department store and got three new outfits. One was a black sheath with a jacket—cocktail dress. The other two were two piece outfits—a pink and a blue. All three together cost $57.00. I also went to the library over in the main hospital. I found about three books on the eye that I think I can get enough material from.

6 Dec 64 Sunday

I worked about three hours on my in-service program. I decided to do it on the anatomy of the eye and general nursing care. I hope it is long enough.

7 Dec 64 Monday

We were up at 3 AM this morning to get ready for Camp Bullis. We left here around 5:45 and got there around 6:45. The first place my group (eleven of us) went was to a Battalion Aid Station. We went out in trucks to this area with nothing there but nature (trees and bushes, etc). We had a truck with the equipment and we had to set it up completely. There were 11 ANCs and about 10 MSCs. We first put up this tent of a pretty large size, then set up places for patients, equipment, a radio set, etc. Patients were brought in on foot and by ambulance. They were taken away by ambulance and by helicopter. At this level you give enough treatment to get the patient to the next place which in most cases is a Clearing Station. The only thing bad about this field exercise is there are no latrines in place and sometimes you wait six or more hours before a latrine break. In the afternoon we tore down, or I should say dismantled and loaded our Battalion Aid Station and were sent to a Clearing Station. Here the tents were up but we set up everything else. This level is where you treat the patient enough to send on. It is mainly a sorting level. Very serious, need of life saving care, and non transportable patients are sent to MASH (a surgical hospital). The others are sent to the evacuation hospital. As of yet, nurses do not work in either the Battalion Aid Station or the Clearing Station so we mainly were there just to get an idea of what happens at these levels. One interesting thing we did—at noon we ate C-Rations. They are a can of main dish. Mine was tuna and noodles. Also I had a can of sea biscuits with peanut butter or jelly. They did not taste very good. Also I had a can with dessert, either fruit or cake (which was pretty hard). All in all it was ok but I wouldn't want to eat it too often or too long. This evening we saw a 2 ½ hour film called "The Long Gray Line." It was the story of a soldier's 50 years in the West Point Academy. It was very good and made you feel good to be in the Army.

8 Dec 64 Tuesday

We got up at 5 AM, had breakfast and got to our new area around 7:15. I worked in a Mash Hospital today. Here we had to set everything up (except the tents). It is a lot bigger than the other two areas. It is equipped to do all surgical cases and all patient care needed. We had to set up the tent we were assigned to with all the cots, make them up, lay out all our paper supplies, equipment, etc. The patients came by way of helicopter and ambulances. We had to (in pre op two) prepare them for surgery and give them care and treatment as needed in our tent. It was interesting and informative. We left about 4 PM for FSH. I'm glad this is the last day at Camp Bullis though I did have a lot of fun and I did learn a lot.

9 Dec 64 Wednesday

My second day in the hospital, mainly I just talked to patients and corpsmen. At 11 AM I had an appointment (which I had asked for) with Major Jamison, the nursing supervisor of Chambers Pavilion which is the psychiatric building at FSH. She was real nice. She gave me a tour of the area and told me a lot about neuro-psych nursing in the Army. I really think that is what I want to do if I can work that out at Fitzsimmons. I might even take the six month NP course offered. This evening was the ANC dress blue banquet. It was held in the large Officer's Club. It started at 7:30 PM with a cocktail hour before. The room was all decked out with red, such as the tablecloths and trimmings. It was very nice with our uniforms of blue. The room was real large and we sat at long tables. For entertainment they had a ventriloquist (one of the MSC students) give an act. He was great. I had heard him once before at the pit. Also, we had group singing. After we went down to the Ravenroom and danced till midnight. I danced mainly with a fellow named Neal. He was 1st Lt. of the Brooks Air force. He wanted to go out after but I have to be up too early for that. The dress uniform looked real nice on. I hope we don't wear them too often because they are rather warm.

10 Dec 64 Thursday
I gave my in-service program. It went pretty well. It lasted about 25 minutes. I think I'll do better next time.

11 Dec 64 Friday
I was head nurse for the half day we spent in the hospital, just for practice. It went ok. This evening Rose and I went to a movie at Lackland AFB Theater. We saw the "7th Dawn." Their theater is nice, about like FSH.

12 Dec 64 Saturday

Today is Rose's birthday. This evening Rose, Rachael and I went to Gray Moss Inn, about 30 miles outside of San Antonio, to celebrate their birthdays which are both in December. During the day, when Rose was gone, a cake came for her from her parents. So I took it and hid it and then when I had a chance I hid it in her car which we were going out in that evening. Once at the Inn I had to sneak it in the back door. It all worked out very well. She was really surprised. We had a real nice party.

13 Dec 64 Sunday

I wrote out all my Christmas cards today. I also attempted to study some for the last exam. It covers all of the nursing material and practice. It alone is worth 400 points of the 1000 points, so I'd better do ok on it.

14 Dec 64 Monday

Well, the exam wasn't easy but maybe I did ok. Rose is going to have another girl plus two enlisted guys driving with her to Nebraska. We went to meet these two guys tonight and through them I met another wanting a ride to Denver and can help Carolyn and I drive. That is good. Now we can drive straight through and have a few days free time to ourselves in Denver before starting to work.

15 Dec 64 Tuesday

We got the results of the exam. I got an A which surprised me. I got 371 points out of 400. So that means I have 3 A's and 1 B for grades which is good. My basic final score of all is 90.4. Larry, the guy riding with me to Denver called and said there was another guy that would like to go. I said ok, only I hope we can get all the luggage in. I've been packing. I sent some of my luggage by shipping. It is really not going to cost very much for gas with four of us splitting it. I called June and Phil this evening to get their address. June was working so I talked to Phil. He is going to send the address home and I'll get it around Christmas.

16 Dec 64 Wednesday

Today is Rachael's birthday. Today in class we got to draw blood on each other. I did it ok. Also, today we had our debridement class on goats. He gave us a demonstration, on incising and debriding a high velocity wound in the leg of an anesthetized goat. Then we split up and two worked on a wound together. We also saw a film and demonstration on doing a tracheotomy. I think I could if I really had too. We also learned very good and important information about mouth to mouth resuscitation and cardiac massage. I really feel this basic course has taught me a lot in first aid and emergency care. I wouldn't feel as insecure now if I happened upon an emergency.

I got a surprise care package from Mrs. Dewey Nelson, Mrs. Schafer, and Mrs. Shawback of the Lostant Methodist Church. It had 2 large cans of cookies, a can of nuts, a can of candy, a box of cookies and candy, hard candy, gum, writing paper, etc. It was very nice to be remembered by them. Now we'll have something to eat while driving to Denver.

17 Dec 64 Thursday
This evening Rose and I went to meet the guys riding with us to our next stations. The two riding with me are Larry and Douglas. They both seem real nice. We all went out for a coke.

18 Dec 64 Friday
Well, you guessed it. Since it was our graduation day it was sleeting and raining and freezing everything. It was really bad out. We had graduation in the theater. It was nice and not too long. It was over by 10:30 AM. We went down to the barracks to pick up the guys around 2 PM, but due to their detail work we didn't leave until around 4:30 PM. I only drove for 2 ½ hours on the whole trip. Otherwise Larry and Doug did all of the driving. For quite a ways the roads were real slick with ice and snow but we had no problems. They drove all night long. Larry invited us out for several days at his home so Carolyn and I went. We arrived at his house around 4:30 PM. His whole family is real nice. It was such a good

feeling to be in a home again especially around Christmas time. This evening Doug and I went out and enjoyed a nice evening.

20 Dec 64 Sunday

Larry asked us to stay over Sunday night too so we will. He gave me a real long ride all over town on a motor scooter. It is the first time I ever rode one and it was fun. The name of the town is Sterling, Colorado. Larry and I washed my car in one of those car washes. This evening Larry and I went out. He insisted we wear uniforms which was ok with me. First we went to a movie. Then we had drinks of coke at the bowling alley. Boy was I stared at everyplace I went. That town has never seen a woman in uniform and it was a novelty to them. It made me very noticed and a little uncomfortable but all in all it was ok. Later we went out to visit his recruiting sergeant. It was a real nice evening. He wants to write so I think it will be fun. Both he and Doug go to Hawaii on 3 Jan 65. They will both be corpsmen.

21 Dec 64 Monday

Carolyn and I left Larry's around 10:30 AM and arrived in Denver around 12:15. We changed into our uniforms before we reported in to our duty station. We reported in around 2 PM and received keys to our rooms. I was quite scared and apprehensive about reporting in and I still am. It is a lot different than FSH. We live in apartment like places. Two girls to an apartment. Each has a bedroom and then shares a bath, living room, and kitchen. The apartment is real nice except there isn't anything such as linens, blankets, dishes, ironing board, soap, paper, etc. I bought an ironing board today. I have everything put away now and am very tired. Good night!!

22 Dec 64 Tuesday

Today we did processing. Running from one place to the other. Boy did my feet hurt. We also get tired much more easily because of the higher altitude. My baggage from FSH came today.

23 Dec 64 Wednesday

Well, today was just one big disappointment. When I woke up I had a terrific sore throat, headache, cold, chills, and dizziness. After we did a little more processing I went on sick call. My temp was 100.8. He gave me a penicillin shot and lozenges. First time I ever had penicillin. He put me on quarters for a few days, probably over Christmas day too. My next disappointment was I am going to work temporarily on pediatrics, of all places. She really picked the one I could do without. My next disappointment was when I got a safety check for my car. Everything was ok except the broken emergency brake. It has to be fixed so I left it overnight at the garage. I sent

Larry's letter off today. I hope he writes back. I put his black tie in that he had left in the trunk and also a thank you note to his mother.

25 Dec 64 Friday

This is Christmas. I reported in to the dispensary in whites. I am not on quarters nor do I have to work today. The chief nurse invited me to come to her office at 11:30 AM to go to the Christmas dinner. That was very thoughtful of her. I am sort of confused as to when to salute her. She seems so friendly and nice that you forget until it is too late. I don't work till Monday. Dinner was real nice and spending it with Colonel Ayers was nice too. Most of the day I've spent reading in my pediatric textbook trying to brush up on it. I called Mr. Ferris—the couple that June knows here in Denver. He answered, she wasn't home. I also found the address of a Baptist church suggested by him that I plan to try Sunday.

26 Dec 64 Saturday

This is the loneliest weekend I've spent in a long time. Being new to a post at Christmas time isn't any fun. No one even knows you are here to invite you to parties if there are any going on. I went to several used car lots today to see how much I would get for my car. They only say $400.00. I am expecting around $900.00 so I'll either sell it privately or try and keep it. It is getting ever so hard to try and pay off my school time debts with these car payments every month. Maybe when I work it won't be so lonely.

27 Dec 64 Sunday
I went to this Baptist church out on Peoria by DelMar. It is a rather small church and most of the people were pretty friendly. I went to Union Training at 6 PM but it was a very small group due to the holidays. I'm ambivalent about starting work tomorrow. In some ways I want to start because I am so lonely not knowing anyone. Well, we'll see. I guess my roommate arrives tomorrow too. I'd rather live alone.

28 Dec 64 Monday
Well, today was my first day in pediatrics. It was mainly getting oriented to the ward. The head nurse and the personnel working there are very nice. I got my Mantoux test today. My new roommate is Diane. She just got married a week ago and her husband is at Fitzsimmons for a few days before he goes to the Dakotas. They are staying at the Officer's Club until then. She seems ok.

29 Dec 64 Tuesday
Today I worked in the preemie room along with the specialist. She was nice and very helpful in orientating me. I learned a lot. There were three preemies. I got a phone in today. I called Bonnie and spoke to her mother because she wasn't

home. Tomorrow I will put an ad in the paper (Stethoscope) about my car. It won't come out until next Friday. I sure hope I get results on it. So far there is no way to meet anybody here. (I am speaking of the male sex.) And almost all of the doctors are married. It has been quite lonely and boring in the evenings with nothing to do. Let us hope things start looking up.

30 Dec 64 Wednesday
I worked in the preemie room alone today. I didn't have any problems. Everything went ok.

31 Dec 64 Thursday
This is New Year's Eve. I had the preemie room again today. It was ok. One interesting thing—This one baby has had all kinds of treatment and formula tried on it and nothing works so they decided to try beer. It's the first time I've ever given beer to a baby. The baby could take one ounce before it got sleepy and stopped. We used Coors beer. I wonder how it will work.

1 Jan 65 Friday
Well, the first day of the new year and I am off. Today at 5:15 PM nursing service was to meet the General at the Officer's Club. Every New Year's Day all officers meet him there. The Officer's Club seemed nice but Carolyn and I didn't stay long. We went to a movie at 7 PM downtown and saw "Mary Poppins."

2 Jan 65 Saturday

I am off today but did not do much of anything. This record book is probably getting pretty boring and I sure hope it gets more interesting shortly. I'm really considering pretty seriously of going overseas. Maybe Hawaii???

3 Jan 65 Sunday

I had medications and treatments today. It was ok. Today was an easy day. Two of the corpsmen working on pediatrics are from Illinois too. One from Galesburg and one from Chicago. There is a civilian nurse that spells her last name exactly like I do. I looked in the Denver telephone directory and there are about 106 parties with the exact same last name as mine.

4 Jan 65 Monday

I am so excited today. I got a lot of mail. I was very surprised and happy to get a letter from Doug. He wrote from Sterling. He says he is going to write me when he gets to Hawaii. He is so nice. I got a gift of a photo book from grandma which is nice. I also got a letter from Lyons. I got a Christmas card from home. The verse was very thoughtful.

It is as follows:

"What happy Christmas we had
When you were a little girl
Who rushed up to the tree
To see your gifts
On Christmas morning!
You looked at each new surprise
With such happiness
Shining in your eyes!
And watching you with a new toy
Brought untold joy to us.
Now that you have grown
To be a lovely young woman,
We think of all the gladness
We've known because of you.
And as we recall those happy years,
We hope the magic of childhood days
Is yours this Christmas morning."

They also sent me a picture of me in my Army uniform that they cut out of the paper.

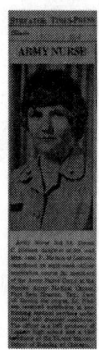

The caption is as follows:
"Army Nurse 2nd Lt. Donna C. Nielsen, daughter of Mr. and Mrs. John F. Nielsen of Lostant, completed an eight week officer orientation course for members of the Army Nurse Corps at the Brooke Army Medical Center, Fort Sam Houston,

Texas, on December 18th. During the course Lt. Nielsen received instruction in performing medical services under combat and disaster conditions. The officer is a 1961 graduate of the Lostant High School and a 1964 graduate of the Illinois Masonic School of Nursing at Chicago."

Today at work I had meds and treatments. It was an easy day. Major York told me they may have to pull me to the TB (tuberculosis) ward for awhile. It might be ok.

5 Jan 65 Tuesday
I am off today. I found out I will start on the TB ward on Thursday. I think it will be ok except that it is a woman's ward and they are always harder to care for. We'll see.

6 Jan 65 Wednesday
I am off today. I was surprised. I got another letter from Doug which he sent out from Oakland, California. He still doesn't have his Hawaii address so he'll write when he does. I am beginning to wonder if I should continue my plans to sign up for Hawaii as overseas duty or not. Because of the problems it might cause over there if we should see each other. Due to the fact that officers and enlisted aren't supposed to fraternize. I also got my income tax papers. I don't know the first thing about them. I also have to fill

out a questionnaire I got from the Masonic Hospital. I wrote a letter to Dolores and asked her to price suitcases for me. I plan to give Mother and Daddy a set of three suitcases. I'll have Dolores buy them for me there. My roommate's name is Diane. I think we will get along fine. Her husband is a horticulturist. He is in South Dakota now, his place of business.

7 Jan 65 Thursday

Today was my first day on the TB wards. At 9 AM I saw the orientation movie that is shown to all new patients. Then I was placed in building 502. TB has three separate areas here at Fitzsimons. 502 is a men's ward consisting of "red suitors." Patients wear red hospital clothes until their sputum is negative for TB for five times. Then they are transferred to building 404 and given blue suits. That is mainly a convalescent ward. The third area is building 403 and that is the woman's ward. They go home after five negative sputum's. Another interesting thing is their setup for wearing of masks for the patients and for the personnel. They have three marked areas called red, white, and blue. The red areas are where the patients sleep, live, and eat. Here the patients do not wear the masks but personnel do if they come in that area. In the blue areas, which mainly are the halls, treatment rooms, etc. the patients wear the masks and the personnel do not. The white areas, such as the kitchen and the nurse's station are off limits to the patients. Personnel do not wear masks in these areas. The head nurse that showed me around today was 2nd Lt. Mary. She is only a year older than I and we got along just fine. Since I only go across the street to work I come home at noon to eat. That should save some money I hope.

8 Jan 65 Friday

Today, mainly I observed at work. I found out I am the only nurse on tomorrow so will be in charge. I hope everything goes ok. I also found out my tentative vacation schedule is May 23rd to June 6th. That includes the extra day of grace. That will make it just a little over 7 months since I was home. A military stand-by ticket from Denver to Chicago via Stapleton Airfield would cost around $60 round trip.

9 Jan 65 Saturday

Today I was head nurse at work. It was very easy today because on Saturday the patients do not have any appointments and nothing else is happening. It was a good feeling though to be in charge. Diane, Carolyn and I went to the post theater and saw "The Grogan." It is so lonely around here with no dating. There is not any place to meet anyone nor are their many bachelors around. Boy, if we could only date enlisted men. I hope Larry or Doug writes again soon. I haven't had any luck selling my car yet.

11 Jan 65 Monday
>   I had meds today. We also had a civil service lecture for orientation to Fitzsimmons General Hospital. I had my second mantoux. Was positive.

12 Jan 65 Tuesday
>   I did meds and generally learned more about the ward. I have a prospect that is going to look at my car on Friday. He is Sgt. Ellis from the ward. I hope he buys it.

13 Jan 65 Wednesday
>   I mainly learned a lot about taking care of the doctor's orders. For the last few days I have been in charge for several hours because the head nurse was away for those times. The patients are real nice and so far all the people you work with in the Army are nice. I got a real big book called Symposium on Pulmonary Diseases. It has everything in it.

14 Jan 65 Thursday
>   Today I worked with the cardex and initialing it. I saw a thoracentesis done too. We had the monthly floor inspection. Boy, everyone worked hard to get a good one. We find out tomorrow what our score was. I was so happy today. I got a letter from Doug from Hawaii. It really sounds beautiful there. I wrote back. Carolyn and I are going to the post theater tonight.

15 Jan 65 Friday
> I was in charge of the floor today and although we were fairly busy everything went fine. I had to go on grand rounds with the doctors and the Colonel. It was my first time and very interesting. They go to each patient and go over his stay in the hospital and ways for improvement.

16 Jan 65 Saturday
> I was off today. Diane and I went for a real long ride clear through Denver and to the foothills. So far the weather has been real good.

17 Jan 65 Sunday
> I was in charge of the floor today. All went fine. This evening Diane and I went to the post theater and saw "How the West Was Won."

18 Jan 65 Monday
> This is my first day on 403 which is the TB woman's ward. It was ok but I like 502 better.

20 Jan 65 Wednesday
> Diane and I went to the post theater this evening.

22 Jan 65 Friday
> Diane and I went to a party given by several of the guys living across the quadrangle. It wasn't any good and we left early.

23 Jan 65 Saturday

I was back on 502 today. One of the new patients, a sergeant gave me a pin he called a crest from when he was in an airborne division. He just came back from Viet Nam. Diane found out her grandmother was very sick so is trying to get leave home.

24 Jan 65 Sunday

Diane's grandmother died early this morning so I took her to the airport at 8 AM. She will return next Friday. This apartment will be rather lonely without her. Tomorrow I work my first day on 404. That is the male convalescent ward or blue suitors. Also the officer red suitors are on that floor. I think I'll like that floor.

25 Jan 65 Monday

My first day on 404. It was a lot of fun and real easy. I worked with a specialist named Harry. He is very nice. He talked with me for about an hour. After work we went to 502 for a birthday party for another specialist. Everybody on duty was there. But best of all I got a letter from Doug. He is very lonely he says and has taken to drinking rather heavy. I wrote a five page letter back.

26 Jan 65 Tuesday

I worked again on 404. It is a lot of fun there. On the day shift we pour 1240 pills. At 502, on the day shift, we pour out 800 pills. That is a lot of pills. I was surprised I got another letter from Doug. He is really lonely. I feel sorry for him. I'll write him back and maybe that will help. I got a letter from Rose and she said she heard from Bob. He told her to say hello to me.

27 Jan 65 Wednesday

I was in charge of 403 for the first time today. It was ok. I also found out I work evenings for 3 shifts next week on 403. I don't care for that.

1 Feb 65 Monday

I was real happy today. I received letters from both Doug and Larry today. I was glad Larry wrote. He said he wrote several before but I did not get them. I paid a $100.00 toward my scholarship loan this month. I hope it doesn't leave me short any. Well better get ready for work. I work evenings for three days this week on 403.

2 Feb 65 Tuesday

I got a letter from Doug today. He fractured his cheek bone. I guess it is pretty sore. His birthday is the 7th of Feb.

6 Feb 65 Saturday

Well, today I decided to trade in my 1960 Ford for a new car. I got a Plymouth Valiant. It is powder blue and should be great. I get it in several days. I had one of the patients from 404 (George) help me find a car. Afterward he took me to supper and then we went to Lookout Mountain. It is really beautiful from there to see all the lights of Denver. He got back an hour late to the ward so got a "DF" written up on him. I hope no one catches us since he is enlisted.

7 Feb 65 Sunday

George and I went to a movie. We went to a drive-in in the middle of winter. They provide car heaters. It was a new experience. Harry and another specialist on 404 are teaching me to play ping pong in our free time at work.

10 Feb 65 Wednesday

There is this one patient on ward 502 named Randy that is really nice. We have talked many times. He is in the process of being transferred either to Hines VA in Chicago or to a State Institute in Chicago. I hope he gets Hines. Anyway, wherever he goes he is going to send me his address and I am going to see him when I go home on leave in May. If he is out of the hospital we are going to see Chicago.

11 Feb 65 Thursday

The guys on 502 are teaching me how to play pool. It is a lot of fun but would take a lot of practice to get good at it.

12 Feb 65 Friday

I got a letter from Rose today. She says Bob

wants to write but won't write first. So I wrote him a letter. It cost him $75.00 to fix his car after he turned it around in San Antonio that night. I also got a letter from Rachael. She likes Letterman and is dating an enlisted man too. I bought Government Personnel Mutual Life Insurance for $12.50 a month. It looks like a real good deal. I hope! I went out with George. First we went and visited a friend and his family. Then we ate something and drove around Denver. He gave me a real big valentine's card and a necklace, both of which surprised me. He says he loves me but I don't believe it. On the valentine's card on the front it says— "You're a very special person. Happy Valentine's Day." Inside the verse is as follows:

> "It's hard to know the phrases
> And all the things to say
> To such a special person
> On this sentimental day
> But somehow it seems only right
> To say, Today of all days
> You're someone close in thought and heart
> Not "now and then" but always!"
> With Love, George

It really was very pretty. I don't know what his plans are. You see he is divorced and has three kids that he is keeping. If his plans are to find a wife, well, that surely is not going to be me. I have no intentions of getting married until after I travel overseas and to different places first. Anyway, I wouldn't want a family already set up for me. He showed me a picture of them, 2 girls and a boy. George's birthday is on Christmas.

13 Feb 65 Saturday
We went down and picked up my new car today. Boy, it runs real well. I am going to pay $55.00 for six months, then $70.00 after that per month. By 6 months I should have my other loans paid off. After, George and I went bowling. I didn't do so well but it was fun learning. Later we tested the car out and drove for awhile. He talks marriage every so often but I've told him he won't get to first base with me.

14 Feb 65 Sunday
George and I went to an indoor movie and then drove around afterwards. The weather was real bad.

15 Feb 65 Monday
I went to personnel and had a $12.50 allotment made out for that insurance. Now I won't have to worry about it each month. I work my first night tonight. I'm not especially looking forward to them. I hope it works out ok. I called USAA in San Antonio and got collision and comprehensive on my insurance put into effect for my new car.

16 Feb 65 Tuesday
   Went out with George for supper. I had to be back early because I was working nights. It was my first night alone but everything went ok.

17 Feb 65 Wednesday
   I got a happy surprise today. I received a refund check for $97.44 which I really needed. I called home too. I received my card on the life insurance. The guys on 502 gave me a big 1 ½ pound box of candy and a valentines card for Valentine's Day. They are so nice to work with. I dropped by 404 to show Harry my new car and played him about six games of ping pong. He and his friend are trying to get me ready to beat Mary. They think I can. Harry said that next week he'll take a ride in my car and said he would buy me dinner too. His friend may come too.

18 Feb 65 Thursday
   My last night. They were not so bad. George asked me to co-sign on his down payment of $320.00 on his car, so I did, with some doubt. We went for a ride and then had supper. Then we went over to 404 and played cards awhile. Bob came and brought a guy named Jim with him. I am going to go out with Bob while he is here. We are going to the "Tiki Kai" on Friday night. Saturday he wanted to take me to the Robin's Nest on Lookout Mountain but I had already made a date with George.

19 Feb 65 Friday
>   Today was supposed to be my day off. But at 7:15 AM I was called and asked to work 403 because several nurses were sick, so I did. That evening at 6 PM Diane and Jim and Bob and I went out first to supper at the "Tiki Kai." Then we were going to see a hockey game but there were no seats left. So we decided to go to the Robin's Nest up on Lookout Mountain but got lost and drove around first. We got there about 10 PM and I did not get home to bed until 1:30 AM. I have to be up at 5:30.

20 Feb 65 Saturday
>   There is another real nice guy on 502 named Park. If he ever gets to 404 we are going to go out sometime. I went out with George tonight. First we went to a movie and saw "36 Hours." Then we went to the "Tiki Kai" for supper. Real nice evening. Got in about 1:30 AM. I've told George to date other girls because I'm not what he wants. He doesn't want too.

21 Feb 65 Sunday
>   This evening Diane cooked supper for Bob and two of his friends—Jim and Cheryl.

22 Feb 65 Monday
>   Harry picked me up from 502 about 10:30 after work and we went out for a hot dog. Then we drove all over Denver. I saw Laramie Street,

some amusement parks and a lot of different places. Had a lot of fun.

24 Feb 65 Wednesday
After I got off at 11 PM Harry and his friend Darrel and his date and I went out.

25 Feb 65 Thursday
I went out with Harry. We drove all over the mountains and saw Central City, Cherry Creek, etc. We met Darrel and Rae and all went to the Aurora Lounge for dancing.

26 Feb 65 Friday
I think I have a problem now. Diane said rumors are about that I am dating enlisted men. I'm not sure what I should do. I don't want to hurt my Army record or career. I went out with Harlan this evening. We saw a movie.

27 Feb 65 Saturday
I went out with Harlan this evening. We doubled with another couple. We went to the Rathskeller. Had fun but I sure am losing out on sleep.

28 Feb 65 Sunday
I went out with Harry this evening. There aren't many places to go on Sunday because the law says no liquor sold after 8 PM and most dance places have liquor.

1 Mar 65 Monday
   I went out with Harry to a movie. We saw "None but the Brave." It was real good and he is really nice.

2 Mar 65 Tuesday
   I and Harlan went to Colorado Springs today. We left about 1300 hours. We stopped by at the Air Force Academy and looked at it. It is big and the grounds are pretty. They have a beautiful church there that we saw. Then we drove in the mountains most of the afternoon. That evening we had a great supper and saw the movie "The Calloways." It was a good day.

3 Mar 65 Wednesday
   I got Colorado license plates today. I had to go clear out to Brighten to get them. The plates cost $45.54 and the Colorado sales tax on my car was 2% so it cost about 42.00. Harry is going to put them on for me tomorrow. Harry and I are going out for a hamburger at 2300 hours after he gets off work. Darrel and Rae might go too. I can't stay out to late because I have to work at 0700 tomorrow.

4 Mar 65 Thursday
   I went out with Harry for dancing at Auroras Lounge. Darrel and Rae were with us too. We had a lot of fun.

5 Mar 65 Friday
>   After I got off work at 2300 hours Harry and I went out for a sandwich and then drove around for awhile.

6 Mar 65 Saturday
>   I got a nice letter from one of my patients on 502 today. It rather surprised me as to his thought about me and his confiding in me. His name is Judson. He is nice but lonely.

13 Mar 65 Saturday
>   Well, I haven't written for a week in here but I've been real busy. I go out most every night sometimes with Harlan but usually with Harry. I'm going to stop writing about every date because that is too much. I'll just write especially interesting places or things we do. Work is going ok. Randy is being sent to the State Hospital in Chicago. He'll be leaving anytime now. We're going to get together when I come home on leave in May. It should be fun.

21 Mar 65 Sunday
>   I decided not to date Harlan anymore because I got word that he talked some in the barracks. I still go out with Harry all the time. Major Dickie told me the other day that I would be assistant head nurse on 502 which is exactly what I wanted. Mary and I will change off weekends. I will work days and some evenings which is fine

with me. I got a letter from Larry yesterday and he still plans on seeing me when he comes home on leave.

23 Mar 65 Tuesday

I was so happy today. Harry got the official word he got the promotion to E-7. For those promotions the man has to go to a board and answer questions on military regulations, current events, and anything the board members decide to ask. He was up against 12–13 others for this same promotion. He got it which is really terrific.

25 Mar 65 Thursday

Personnel called today and told me I could go to Germany next September if I wanted too. Both Harry and Randy don't want me to go. I'll think about it but really think I will. That is what I joined the Army for.

26 Mar 65 Friday

Today Harry gave me a surprise. That morning he received his E-7 stripes from Colonel Taylor. He gave me those stripes which was really nice.

Here is a copy of the letter of recommendation given for and to him by Major Dickie of TB services.
1. As senior Hospital Medical Assistant on the TB service for the past seven months, your performance of duty has been outstanding.

2. You have shown a keen interest in your work and have cooperated fully with the professional nursing staff to provide the optimum in patient care. You have been observant and inquisitive, constantly seeking ways to increase your medical knowledge and skills.
3. You have established good relationships with your co-workers as well as with the patients, at the same time maintaining the discipline necessary to the smooth operation of a mixed ward of officers and enlisted men.
4. Your enthusiasm and your untiring effort have been greatly appreciated by all who have had the privilege of working with you. I am requesting that a copy of this letter be placed in your military 201 file.

        June M. Dickie
        Major ANC
        TB Nursing Supervisor

Now he is working as ward master on 4E which is in the recovery room.

30 Mar 65 Tuesday

I don't really know how to say this. Crying didn't help and writing it is harder. I am so sad. Harry wrote me a letter as follows:

My Darling Donna,
"Before I start this I want you to know that deep in my heart I don't really want to even write this

but it will be easier on me in the future if I do it now. The other night I told you a lie or a fib, however you want to look at it. I love you very much Donna and I told you that I didn't want to get serious with you and that I would never get taken again, meaning married. I didn't want to say that but at the time I thought it would be best for both of us if I did. I know now that you could never love me and I am no good for you. I don't want to get you in trouble with anybody by you going out with me. The only difference that I can see between us is that I am a divorcee and you have never been married. Age to me means nothing. Its all how one feels towards each other. I don't need to tell you how much I love you and want to be with you every minute of each day. It will be easier on me to give you up now then keep going with you until September and then have to say goodbye to you. I have been hoping that maybe, by some small miracle, that you would change your feeling toward me and that we could make a go of things. However, since you have definitely said that you will go to Europe in September and that that is why you came in the Army, I know where I stand. Since I first met you, you have been something, something special to me. Something that I could look up to with the deepest respect. I will never lose my respect or love for you. It is hard for me to write this because I have never had to write something like this before. If at any time you need me you know where you can get me. I have enjoyed every minute with you and only hope you feel the same about being with me. You are a very sweet person and I hope you find happiness throughout your life. What happens to me from now on only time will tell. I thought when I met you that I had found what I had been looking for but I guess, as usual, I was wrong. Please don't take that sentence the wrong way. You are what I have been looking for but I know that I could never have you as my own. There are so many things that I had planned for us this summer especially if I got that promotion, but now I guess it doesn't really matter. As I told you before I might be wrong in writing this and I hope I am. If you want to talk to me please feel free to call me or write me a letter and give it to me. I'll never forget you Donna as long as I live. I only hope that you can find a small place in your heart to remember me."

All My Love Forever,

Harry

P.S. "Believe me, I don't want it this way and maybe you can show me a better solution."

1 April 65 Thursday

Harry called and wanted to see me so we had a long talk. He asked me to marry him but I can't give him an answer as yet. I don't know.

3 April 65 Saturday

I talked over many things with Harry this evening.

4 April 65 Sunday
I told Harry I would marry him. I do love him and hope everything will work out. He wants me to wait before we make plans until I go home on leave and talk to my folks. Also, he has to see about getting a transfer overseas. He knows several Colonels that may help him.

5 April 65 Monday
I wrote a long letter home telling them all about Harry and our plans. I hope they are in favor of it. I can only wait to hear from them now.

6 April 65 Tuesday
Harry wants to add all our debts together and then borrow a lump sum from the bank. Then we would only have to make one payment a month of around $70.00. I think it is a good idea. He plans to sell the VW and that would pay quite a lot on my car. It was rather funny. Yesterday, Harry got my mail and in it was a letter from Doug. He was pretty curious as to who Doug was, so I told him about Doug, Larry and Bob. I'm not sure what he thought.

7 April 65 Wednesday
Harry and I broke up. I hope it is for the best. He was very hurt and I am really sorry. He was

mad too because I was going to date other guys. I realize I do not feel I can lead him on under false pretenses.

8 April 65 Thursday
I went out with Randy. We went to the mountains and to Central City. We had a real nice time. He is so nice.

9 April 65 Friday
Randy and I went to a drive-in movie. He says he loves me but I've warned him I am going to Germany this September. He doesn't listen to that.

12 April 65 Monday
I had to go to the dentist today. I had one filled and he pulled the upper one—last tooth on the right side. It isn't too bad so far.

15 April 65 Thursday
Randy went to the hospital for hernia surgery. I also told him I couldn't date him anymore because I was spoken to about dating patients. The Easter Bunny (Harry) sent me a candy Easter basket and a pot of Lilies. First time I ever had flowers. I still don't know what is going to happen between us.

16 April 65 Friday
I had the TB in-service meeting today. I had Dr.

Spatwitz to give a talk. He showed slides and talked on Yokohama Asthma. Around 4:30 I went up to the hospital to visit Randy. He was real surprised to see me as I had told him before that I probably couldn't come up.

17 April 65 Saturday
    It was Darrell and Rae's wedding today at 4:00. It was a nice ceremony. Then afterward was a reception at their apartment. Around 8:30 PM Harry and I left and went where we could talk. I told him I planned on dating other guys. He does not believe in this and said he would not date me if I did. So I guess I will not be seeing him.

29 April 65 Thursday
    I guess I have been neglecting to write in here quite a bit lately. I really have been pretty busy. I have had a lot to think about. As I told Harry I was going to date other guys. I went out with Chris once but doubt if I do again even though he wants too. Mainly I've been dating Randy. We have a lot of fun. But so far I find Harry the most considerate of me and loves me the most. I found out he bought me a wedding gift. It is a brand new house being built in Colorado Springs. It has a fireplace, a 2 car garage, 4 bedrooms, a rec. room, and many other added features. It cost around $17,000.00. I went out with him for the first time since the wedding on Saturday the 17th. We went to a movie and saw "David & Lisa"

and "Lord of the Flies." He goes in the hospital today because he is going to have a hernia surgery on Friday. We're going to go out tonight if he gets a pass. I'm going to visit him in the hospital too.

7 May 65 Friday

I have a little catching up to do in this book. Last week Randy bought me a real pretty cross (gold necklace). He also gave me the old silver necklace he always wore. I had to tell him I wouldn't be able to date him anymore. Partly because of him being a patient but mainly because Harry didn't like it and I really do like Harry. I have been giving marriage to him a lot more thought. Last Sunday Harry and I drove to Colorado Springs and up in the mountains. We went to Bear Trap Ranch (that is the camp I was at 3 years ago in high school). It still looks the same and was real nice to see again. That evening in Colorado Springs he showed me the Army Post (Fort Carson). He took me through a model home like the one he had bought me. Really nice. He also showed me the plot of ground where his house will stand. His operation turned out fine. He is ok. Dolores sent me a letter saying the suitcases arrived and are nice. I hope so. Several girls on "Strac" got a six hour notice to leave for the Domninican Republic last week. It keeps you wondering if you're going to be called or not. I received orders the other day saying that I have to report into Fort Dix, New Jersey on September 13, 1965. I can take a 30 day leave before but I probably won't take more than 15–20 days. I also got my TB test this last week. I was happy it turned out to be negative. Harry was glad too.

29 May 65 Saturday
I guess I really haven't kept up this book very well, so I'll write quite a lot on what has happened. On May 21 I told Harry that I wouldn't marry him now. That I just didn't love him. I really think a lot of him but that isn't enough. I went on leave May 23rd and will be on it till June 6th. I drove home by myself. On the way home I was gone 27 hours and drove 20 of those. It was a thousand miles all together. It was a real long trip and I was really tired when I got home. I spent the 26th and 27th up at Johnny's. I stayed that one night out at Bonnies. She is to be married on June 26th. That day I went to see Randy because we were going to go out in Chicago but the State Hospital said he had to stay there at least until his records came. We were really disappointed but we are going to write. I have heard from Harry several times (2 letters and 2 phone calls). He misses me so much. I miss him too. He is really nice. He has helped me on so many problems as I will relate soon. He found out on his court hearing about his divorce that he

has to take a 60 day continuance. He was rather depressed about that.

Now I will relate a deal that has bothered me for the last couple months now.

On the 18 Feb 65 I signed a loan amounting now to $347.00 for George. It was a down payment for his new 65, tan, 2 door, Valiant. I didn't think anymore about it till about a month and a half ago when the loan company called me and told me he had not paid and they did not know where he was. I right away called the personnel and found out he was at the Denver VA Hospital. I also called Harry and asked him to help me. Harry and I and a guy from the loan company went to the VA Hospital and they talked to him. He promised to pay but never did. About 3–4 weeks from this date I got a call from the finance company and they told me I was signed for the whole car too, which I did not know. This now amounted to $1937.00 on the car and they wanted their money too. So altogether the 2 debts added to $2285.40. Darrel checked around for me because we couldn't find George since the VA Hospital had released him. We found out he was in Illinois where he originally comes from. We got 3 addresses in Illinois from the VA Hospital. The plan was since the finance company said I had repossession rights of his car, was that I get the necessary papers and repossess the car when I went on leave to Illinois. I never would have tried to take it alone but would have had a deputy to go with me. As it worked out about 5 days before my leave Darrel found out he was back in Denver. So we found the address of his girlfriend and through her found out where he worked. So on Thursday May 20th, Darrel and I went down to that place of work to see him. We gave him a choice—either that he get someone to sign for the whole loan and give Darrell a call by 2 PM the next afternoon or I would repossess the car. So he never called, so the next day which was a Friday, I and Harry and a guy from the finance company went to his place of work to retake the car. I knew we would have trouble with him and we did. But after about 3 phone calls he had to give the car to the finance company to hold. The finance company gave me their word that (since I was going to leave on Saturday) they would either keep the car till I got back or George made a full payment. I went on leave May 23rd. On May 25th Harry called as planned to tell me about the meeting between George and the district manager of the company on that day, but George never showed up. On the 27th, a Thursday, after I got home from Chicago they said Harry had tried to call me so I called him back. He told me George had given up the car completely so it is all mine now. Harry also said he and Darrel and Diane would try to sell it for me and advertise it in the post newspaper. I really hope they can. I'll see what happens when I get back. Mother can lend me $700 dollars if I need it to pay on the car. So much for this now. I'll write more on it as I find out.

June and Phil were here at our house the 29-30 of May. Willa also dropped in too.

THAT IS THE END OF MY WRITINGS IN THE GREEN RECORD BOOK!

The end of my record book leaves a few things up in the air.

Mother and Daddy ended up bailing me out of the car. Mother came out to Denver and drove the car back home. They bought it. It may have been one of the first new cars they ever owned. Anyway, another hard life lesson learned.

While mother was in Denver, she met Harry. She advised me against him because of his age (12 years older) and the wife and children from which he was divorced. I expect that played a major role in my decisions later.

As far as Harry goes, we kept dating until I left for Germany. I said I would return to him but he knew better. He knew once I went away I would never be back. And that is what happened as later writings will tell you. Who knows what would have happened to my life if we had stayed together. (Harry also tried to get in touch with me years later when I was divorced, but Mother would not give him my address or phone number). She also never told me that he tried to contact me until years after that. Maybe if we had stayed together my life would have been better. As it was, I sure made bad choices in many, many ways and led a tough adult life due to my poor decisions and choices. I really made a mess of my life.

Mother and Daddy raised me right and gave me the skills and morals to live a good life. I just turned away and did not use them. I held to my upbringing and morals as far as sex was concerned, but that did not help me make any better choices in love and marriage. Actually, in later life, I did not hold closely to my upbringing as I should have.

As my life turned out, I definitely could have done better. My work record was always good. It was my choices in my first and second marriages that left a lot to be desired, but I will get to that in future writings in this narrative.

I wanted to add another thought or two about the green record book. When I read it, as I was writing this narrative, I was amazed about how much dating I had done. I had never dated until I came into the Army. The way it looks, I did not always use good judgment. I was not as mature as I probably thought I was and did not make good decisions even back then. I guess they say, "Live and learn," but on reflection, I sure wish I had done many things differently. Basically I am a good person, but many times in my life, I have not held to the standards that I should have.

HEIDELBERG, GERMANY

My next duty station after I left Denver, Colorado, was overseas in Heidelberg, Germany. Since I was an officer, I was able to take my own car with me. I drove it to New York to be shipped overseas and picked up at the port in Bremerhaven, Germany. This car was a Valiant.

I wish I had continued to keep the record book all of the time I was in the Army, but I did not. Therefore, many things may seem very sketchy in this writing.

I was stationed at the 130th Station Hospital in Heidelberg. I lived in a BOQ, which stands for Bachelor Officer Quarters. It was a two-room and bath apartment, which I had to myself. It was actually down the road from the hospital a fair piece, so it was good that I had my car for transportation.

At the hospital, I worked on male wards usually. I was assigned to two wards—a med-surg ward and an orthopedic ward. Sometimes I was assigned as supervisor of the hospital for my shift. I usually worked the evening shift. Sometimes I would be on the night shift.

We also had times they would call us up at the BOQ in the middle of the night with orders to meet at the hospital and go out on a field exercise. This consisted of going out on the trucks with all of our gear and in our fatigue uniform and boots. We would set up a field hospital and stay there a few days operating this hospital. You never knew when this would happen.

Most of this account will not pertain to my actual work in the Army, but will lean more toward my personal life and travels. I will talk about the various places of travel, though they may not be in order of when they were made. I still have stories about some of these travels. I was stationed in Heidelberg, Germany, from the fall of 1965 until around mid-year or the fall of 1967.

LEONARD

I met Leonard as a patient on the orthopedic ward. He was very handsome and had a very nice personality. We really got along well. He was in the hospital because a 500-pound bomb had rolled across his wrist when he was helping to unload the bombs. At first they didn't realize that he had a fracture, so it was left unattended for some time. As it turned out, he had a fracture on the navicular bone in his right hand. When I met him, he had a cast on his right arm. He was also right-handed, but the cast did not get in his way.

When he got out of the hospital, he was assigned to the armory. He could do that job with the limited use of his right hand. He enjoyed that duty.

We dated for awhile, got along well, and enjoyed each other's company. We decided to get married and went together to talk to our Commanding Officers. They tried to talk us out of it, but we were adamant. They finally capitulated.

We actually had two weddings. The first was

by the German government and the second by the American chaplain on base.

The German wedding was in a room much like a small courtroom. That may have been what it was. A justice of the peace or maybe a judge actually married us. It was very quick and functional. We did have this couple we were friends with stand up for us as our witnesses. The German wedding was actually the legal wedding.

We had the American wedding at the chapel on base and an Army chaplain did the honors; the same couple stood up for us there. I believe Lee's CO was there too. Of course, we did not have any family or other friends there.

I expect Mother and Daddy were not really in favor of this wedding but were too far away to be able to discuss it with us.

We had to find living quarters off base, and we found a nice apartment in Mannheim, Germany. This was a small town close to Heidelberg.

I was probably a 1st Lt. by then, and I believe Lee was a Spec. 5.

We got along great. Lee was very good to me and respected me. He was a very gentle person. He never used bad or foul language. He did smoke cigarettes (Lucky Strikes) but used very little alcohol. I did not drink or smoke then or ever in my lifetime. We set up our apartment and had friends. We went out some to places in town or on base. We enjoyed being with each other and doing things together. We neither one made much money, but we lived on what we had.

TRAVEL IN EUROPE

We both loved to travel, and since that was my main objective in going overseas, we did as much as we could on a "shoestring." I had my car, which we used everywhere we went. I had to do all the driving as Lee could not get a driver's license in Germany. I don't remember why now.

We did not always think our travel through as well as we could have, as will be indicated in several of my stories. We sometimes did not use common sense. We were young and believed we were infallible.

We went on our honeymoon to Denmark. It was a very brief visit. We put the car right on the ferry and rode across on the ferry with it, but when we got to Copenhagen, the gas price was so high ($1.00 a gallon) that we could not afford to stay there long. At that time, that price was very high.

So we finished our honeymoon in a place called Travemunde. It was a coastal town I believe, as I remember water and boats. We enjoyed our stay there and then realized when we got back home that we could have been in big trouble. Germany has the five demilitarized zones that you are not allowed to cross. I don't even remember what it was all about, but we were across it the whole time. If we had been caught, I don't know what would have happened.

Another trip we took was to Berlin. We were foolish and not thinking and could have been in serious trouble two times on this trip. It is a wonder we ever survived Europe.

When we were driving towards Berlin, we came to checkpoints. At the first checkpoint, they stopped us and checked our ID and the car. They told us exactly what speed we had to drive to the next checkpoint and told us that we could not leave the road for any reason. They said if we drove too fast we would reach the checkpoint too quickly. If we drove too slowly, then someone would come looking for us.

Well, we set out and did all that okay. We got to Berlin and found a hotel. Then we decided, since it was nighttime, to go to a movie. Here we were—in a city where no one knew us or knew that we were there.

While we were watching the movie, we heard our names called over the loudspeaker requesting us to come to the lobby. We did, and they escorted us to another place in town—like a police station. Evidently, somehow we had missed the final checkpoint at Berlin. We never did know how we could have missed it. We also did not know how they could have found us, but they did. They let us off with a warning and let us continue our vacation.

We decided to take a trip into East Berlin. (This was when the Berlin Wall was still standing and very much in force.) They had guard towers with armed troops in them. All across the top of the wall were pieces of glass and rock and barbed wire. We had to go through a checkpoint. We were on a city bus. They ran mirrors under the bus and also came aboard to do random checks on the passengers.

In East Berlin, we went to the war memorial park. We were in uniform. It seems to me that when we traveled we were required to wear our uniforms. I remember we had our picture taken with several Russian soldiers in this park. A person from *Look* magazine took the picture and said she would send us a copy. (Many months later we were surprised to receive this copy).

East Berlin was bleak and had very little pedestrian traffic. On both sides of the Wall, you could see bullet holes in some of the buildings.

We got on the bus to return back to the Wall when we realized that we had left all of our actual ID in our hotel room. We were really sweating it; we could be asked for it on the return check at the wall. We were concerned about causing some international incident. Thank goodness we made it across safely.

Another trip that we took was to Paris. We saw a lot of things there. The one thing I remember was how dirty the streets were, and there were guys carrying sides of beef right through the streets. Dogs were running loose, and there were lots of flies.

We went to the top of the Eiffel Tower. We rode up in this really rickety, old elevator that made you wonder if you would make it. There were three levels, and we got off at each of the levels and took pictures of the city. I still have all of those pictures. The view from the top was stunning.

We went to the Louvre. We, of course, saw the Mona Lisa, and I was able to take a photo of her, which I still have. We saw the Arch of Triumph. I am sure that if I had kept a record of this trip there would be many more things to report.

Another thing we did in France was to visit Raymond in a small mining town. Raymond is my brother John's son. Raymond went to France to live when he was a baby, and John's ex-wife moved back there. When we saw him, he was maybe 4–5 years old and had bright red hair. We were only there a few hours and talked mainly with Lilly, his mother.

One big trip that we took was to Rome. We went down through Switzerland. We rode a train through a mountain. It was a long ride and our car was on this train too. I no longer can tell you where we were.

We stayed in Rome and saw so many sights that I cannot begin to recount all the places we went. We saw the Roman ruins, the catacombs, the coliseum, the Sistine Chapel ceiling and so much more. We saw the Vatican but did not go inside. I bought my aunt Dolores a religious medal there that was supposed to have been blessed by the Pope. If I ever have a chance to return to Europe, Rome is where I would want to go. I feel that now I would have a much deeper appreciation and understanding for what I was seeing. I would be more aware of all of the fine art and places that we saw.

We went to Florence and stopped there for a night or two. The memory that has stuck with me for all of this time is about our first night. As soon as we got into our hotel, we decided to go out on foot and walk around town. We walked a long time, and then realized we had lost our hotel and did not even remember the name. We spotted a taxi, and he was able to help us find it by our description. So much for common sense.

We went to Venice. (You park outside of Venice.) We ate lunch there, and the waitress gave me a tiny glass deer for eating in her restaurant. I still have it. We did not ride a gondola but walked over the bridges and saw them and saw other people in them. The buildings rise right up out of the water. It is so different from anything I have ever seen. It also is the only place where we had forgotten to take our camera, so I did not get any pictures of Venice.

We came back through Austria. Since I had to do all the driving, I remember being on those mountaintop roads at night. It was so cold and icy and snowy—not to mention the straight-down cliffs. It probably would have been even more frightening if we could have seen where we were going.

Speaking of driving, it is so different in Europe. In Germany, they had the autobahns that did not have any speed limits. Everyone drove so fast. In Paris and Rome especially, the city traffic was terrible. We would get in these big circles and go around and around because the traffic was so tight and fast that we couldn't get out.

In Heidelberg, we saw the Heidelberg Castle, which was quite interesting. There were many castles throughout Germany. We also saw beautiful, big German military cemeteries. The other main memory I had of Germany was the good food. They had great restaurants and bakeries.

TO THE STATES

We were married less than a year when Lee got orders to return to the states, but I did not. This might have partly been done to discourage marriage between officers and enlisted.

Lee was sent back to Fort Hood, Texas. I put in requests to be sent back too—but to no avail. We wrote letters and had a few phone calls, but it was a very hard time for us both. When Lee went back, he stopped by my folks and visited with them. That was probably rather hard to do by himself.

I was sent back to Fort Hood, Texas, in the mid-year to fall of 1967. I worked in the hospital there in the orthopedic unit while awaiting my normal discharge at the end of October of 1967. I had made captain before I left Europe. Reflecting back, we should have stayed in the military and retired from there. Yet we did not because we felt we did not want to be separated all of the time.

We rented a place to live in Killeen, Texas. We did a lot of sight-seeing around Texas. Lee got a motorcycle, and we rode it all over Texas on our days off. It was a lot of fun, but we got very bad sun and windburns. Lee and I were still doing great together and really enjoyed each other's company.

Lee was a natural-born artist and could draw pictures, caricatures, cartoons, cars, or anything else. He could have studied and worked in art if he had wanted to.

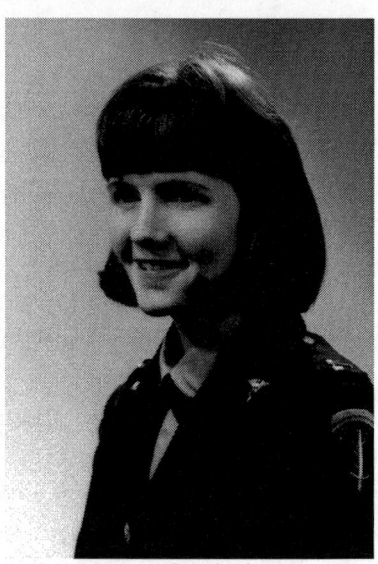

My Army Captain picture.

Chapter Four - Civilian Life

OHIO

When we were both discharged from the Army with honorable discharges, we went to Blacklick, Ohio, near Columbus, Ohio. This was in Oct. of 1967. Lee had a sister and her family living there. I was able to get a nursing job immediately and do not really remember what type of nursing I did there. It may have been a med-surg floor. Lee never worked there.

I don't know why, but we moved to Akron, Ohio. It was where his mother lived with her husband. Lee's father had died prior to my knowing him. Again, I found a nursing job immediately while Lee did not work.

I don't recall when exactly, but in 1968, we packed up all of our belongings in a U- Haul and set out for California. Maybe a completely new start would help our now foundering marriage. As long as we were in the service, Lee had a job and a paycheck. Once he got out of the military, he did not have any desire to work at a real job.

We did not have any specific destination in mind in California. We decided we would stop when we saw what we wanted. We drove through Sacramento, California, and thought that was a possible.

However, we decided to go on to San Francisco and check that out first.

We arrived in San Francisco at night and got on those great big hills, up and down, pulling our U-haul and decided that was not for us. We could not take too long to make a decision as we were about out of money. We stayed that night in San Francisco and decided to head back to Sacramento. On the way back, we stopped for gas in Stockton, California. That looked like a really nice town to call home.

Our first few nights were in some dirty, old downtown hotel. Then we looked at a trailer park and found this tiny trailer for rent. We took that. At the same time, I had already started work in a hospital on a med-surg floor. For the first 2–3 weeks, we lived on potatoes until my first paycheck came through.

I worked at this hospital for a while before taking a job at a very small community hospital in Lodi, California. At this hospital, I worked med-surg and also was responsible for a tiny emergency room. My most memorable experience in this ER was a young woman who had caught her foot in the propeller of a boat. She had very deep slashes in her foot. We did not have a doctor there all the time, so we had to call one to come in.

During all of this time, Lee and I also enjoyed sight-seeing and going to the mountains. Over these years, Lee became interested in Jeeps, so we had several jeeps. He had guns and reloading equipment and even cast his own bullets. He had CB radios, both baseline and for the autos. He belonged to all of the clubs associated with each of these interests.

The one thing he did not have any desire to do was to work and hold a job. Granted, he still was going to the VA hospital for his wrist, which never did heal as long as I knew him. Part of this was because he did not pay attention to the doctor's advice not to use his right hand. He took motors in and out of his Jeep and used it for everything he wanted. That may have been why it did not ever heal.

I offered him a chance to go to college and to get an education. He had gotten his GED in the Army. He did not want to do that either. So ultimately, during our 6 1/2 years of married life he never really worked after he got out of the military. This was to become a major factor in our divorce later on. I was partly to blame. I made mistakes, too, during the time I was married to Lee.

I will depart from discussing our marriage to fill you in on another job that I had while in Stockton.

JAIL NURSE—CALIFORNIA

In the late '60s or early '70s, I saw an ad in the paper for a jail nurse. This caught my eye as being a very unusual and interesting career choice. So I went on several interviews at the hospital that was given the job of finding a jail nurse. The jail had never had a nurse before, just a doctor that came once a day for sick call. Then the deputies did their best to carry out his orders.

I was selected and started work. There was no job description, as it had not ever been done before. So it was up to me to create the whole job and figure out the best way to carry it out. The jail (San Joaquin County Jail) had three sections on the compound. The big main men's jail had two tiers of prisoner cells. On the bottom floor was all of the offices including my office, cooking facilities, and the visiting area. The next building a little distance away was the women's jail. It was a one-story building; otherwise, the set up was similar. I had an office there too. The last building was even further away. This was the honor farm. I also had an office there.

We started at 6 a.m. every morning, Monday through Friday. The doctor arrived, and we held sick call in each of the three buildings. He checked each patient, and I assisted with any exams. He ordered any medication that was required and specified the dosage the patient was to be taking for the duration of the time the patient was in the jail. If patients had to be sent to the hospital, either the deputies transported them or an ambulance came and took them to the San Joaquin County Hospital. It was several miles away from the jail compound.

After the doctor left, I was there to set up packets of medication for the deputies to give out daily. I found that I could use these small coin envelopes to keep the daily medications secure after I sealed them. I spent hours typing on each packet what the medication was, the instructions on how to take it, and the patient's name. For all three jails, I typed up hundreds of these. On Friday, I prepared three days worth to carry over the weekend. If an inmate was released prior to the time the prepared packet of medication was taken, then the packet was returned to me, and I placed the medication back into our supply. This happened very often.

I devised a method of ordering inventory and restocking all of our common medications, ointments, dressings, and all manner of other supplies for all three jails.

Our equipment was rather primitive. When I first started, I had a small oblong sterilizer that I used to sterilize needles, instruments, and syringes. We used the same equipment over and over. This was before disposable, prepackaged syringes were available for use at the jail.

I had to scrounge typewriters and all of the paper supplies and equipment I needed for each clinic. The chief of the jail and all of the deputies were very helpful in getting all of this established. The job also involved training the deputies in various aspects. I gave in-service programs and was always available for any questions.

Many times they would bring an inmate in to see me with some complaint or other. The doctor gave me a lot of freedom, and I had a list of standing orders that I could use. If a patient came in presenting certain symptoms or problems, I could initiate treatment and then the doctor would see the inmate on sick call the next day. If I decided a patient needed to be seen at the hospital right away, I sent them.

Many times I would be called in emergency situations to go up to the tiers or to the drunk tank to see an inmate too severe to be brought to my office. These problems could include anything from delirium tremens (DTs), seizures, heart attacks, suicide attempts, hangings, stab wounds, fights, or any other severe medical problem. I was also called to the other two jails for emergencies. I would drop everything and respond immediately.

We had a lot of seizure-related incidents, as we had many inmates going through DTs and some inmates with epilepsy. They would get off their medications on the outside, and then when they were booked again, they would be brought in and would be in serious trouble. This happened over and over again.

I worked at the jail about 3 ½ years. Over that time, I got to know many of the inmates very well. They were often repeaters and came back many times.

I kept a card on each inmate listing the name, the medical problems, the medications they needed, and everything else about them that I would need to know each time I would see them. When they came in, they were brought to see me so that I could get them started right away on their medications.

We had drunks who had been found in fields. Several come to mind. One had a foxtail stuck in his eardrum. Another had maggots in his ear. They all came smelly and unwashed, clad in dirty clothes, and reeking of alcohol and vomit. We also had inmates come in going through withdrawals from drug abuse.

Many times I felt that the only thing that kept them alive was returning to the jail and getting on medication again.

The first few years I was there, I pretty much had the run of all three jails. If called to any of them for an emergency, I could go myself. I would go up on the tiers to a cell and handle the situation. The deputies had to buzz me through all the doors so they would know I was there.

One day we had a riot. The inmates rioted in the main men's jail. They began breaking things and starting fires. We had deputies on the roof with guns and shields as well as all over the jail. Many were called to come in from home.

I stayed in my little office working as I always had so much work to do. I often worked 10–12 hours a day to keep up. I stayed in my office until the tear gas started seeping under my door. At that point, I had to leave and go outside. I stayed around in case any injuries to deputies or inmates needed to be attended to. The riot lasted well into the night and maybe as long as several days. I do not recall exactly how long now. I know that they got them out into the exercise yard and then under lockdown.

I guess there had been rumor of them trying to take the nurse hostage. So after that riot, I always had to have a deputy go with me to the tiers or into a cell or a drunk tank. That was probably safer.

I want to relate several stories that happened while I worked there.

This was during the time of the Manson murders in LA. One day a female inmate was brought into my office. It was Squeaky Fromme. She was one of the Manson girls and had tried to assassinate President Ford, I believe.

There was this male inmate who was an alcoholic and a repeater that came back many, many times. He was always brought into the main jail in terrible condition. He also was an epileptic. I'll call him Ralph.

Over the years I got to know him very well. He used to help out in the clinic at the honor farm with various jobs. After I left the jail and went elsewhere, I heard that he cleaned up his act, married a nurse, and was working in a rehabilitation-type unit. I always thought he was one of my success stories.

Another inmate that was a junky was also a repeater. A few years after I left the jail, I wrote a story about this particular inmate for a college writing contest. This story was published in a small book of winners. The book was titled "College Contemporaries—Short Shorts and Poetry". It is a semi-annual magazine for and by college students. My story was published in Volume 1, December 1976.

My story as published is as follows:

RONNIE

I really didn't want to become a nurse. But I couldn't let my family down: my mother was a nurse and so was my older sister. So after three years of training, studying, and hospital work, I ended up with an R.N. diploma and—a job at the county jail.

Ronnie was one of my first cases of heroin addiction. I remember him well as he stood or rather slouched before me in my office. He was trembling, with heavy perspiration beading his forehead, his eyes red and watering, his nose running. He looked as lousy as he said he felt. He was complaining of severe abdominal pain, cramping in his back and leg muscles, and aches and pains throughout his body.

"I can't stand it anymore. Please send me to the hospital," he begged. "I can't go back to that cell. I can't take it."

I felt sorry for him, but sympathy cannot play a part in some cases. I held out a Thorazine 75 mg. to him.

"Take this. Just take a little water or you'll lose it. It isn't necessary to send you to the hospital. I'll bring around another pill this evening. You will be given this medication for three days to help you." It wouldn't really do that much for him. I knew this, and he probably did too.

The next day he appeared like a drug-out weak kitten.

"I feel like hell. Those —dam pills didn't help. I didn't get any sleep. I can't eat. I want to go to the hospital."

"I'm sorry Ronnie. The hospital will not give you anything more than I have. It just isn't necessary to send you over."

Ronnie turned to the deputy. "I want to see the Lieutenant."

The deputy looked questioningly at me.

I said, "That's fine, let him see the lieutenant if he wants." I knew the lieutenant would see him, but I also knew that he would ask me about his case and would not send him if I didn't feel he need be. Sure, Ronnie felt miserable, but what could you expect coming off a $100.00 a day heroin habit. He would feel rocky for three of four days and still feel lousy for several weeks.

For Ronnie the weeks went by during which he went to court and received his sentence. He was a rather chronic physical complainer and always had something wrong with him. During the next several months I got to know him fairly well.

He had problems in jail. Due to his small stature he was approached several times indecently by other inmates. This can be a traumatic experience for any young fellow.

One particular morning he was on the sick call list. When his turn came, the doctor inquired, "What's your problem, son?"

Ronnie was hesitant, probably because I was in the room. He mumbled something.

The doctor said, "Speak up, I can't hear you."

"Three of them got me last night. It hurts and was bleeding last night."

The doctor was adjusting a light on one side of the clinic. "Take down your pants and bend over so I can examine you."

"I can't with her here." He didn't move.

"She's a nurse. She's seen this before."

I turned my back to give him the privacy he felt he needed. When the doctor was finished, he gave him a tube of antibiotic ointment with instructions to apply it.

Turning to the deputy, the doctor said, "Can this boy be moved to a cell by himself for awhile?"

The deputy indicated this would be taken care of.

Several weeks later his name came up before the Chief as a candidate to go to the honor farm. There he would have more freedom to move around the compound. He could enter into a work furlough program and maybe serve his sentence easier.

I saw him down at the honor farm too, as he still had the same physical complaints. He often came in just to talk to me while I was working. By this time we knew each other pretty well, and I maintained an interest in his progress.

One day I came to work and found he had been transferred back to the main jail. On questioning the deputy in charge of the honor farm, I was told, "We caught him last night with a set-up, an eyedropper and a needle. He was higher than a kite."

The next few days he was pretty sick again, and we went through the same routine as before.

Several weeks later I was at the female jail when one of the deputies called me.

"The main jail wants you immediately. They have an emergency."

Never knowing what to expect, whether it could be a seizure, a hanging, a heart attack, or some other thing, I ran all the way back. Coming in the booking door, I was let through the locked doors by a deputy.

"There, in your office. He slashed his wrists."

I felt a little relieved it wasn't any more serious. Going into my office, I saw Ronnie and a deputy with him trying to stem the flow of blood. There was blood all over his clothes, all over the towels wrapped around his arms and splattered on the white porcelain sink.

"What happened, Ronnie?" It was just a question to open a conversation if he wanted to talk.

"I didn't want to live. My life is so messed up. I guess I can't even kill myself right."

After cleaning off some of the blood, I determined the cuts were deep enough to require suturing, which meant he had to be sent to the hospital.

"Ronnie, I'm going to put a bandage on and send you to the hospital for stitches. I'll contact Dr. Adams, our psychiatrist, to talk with you when you return."

Ronnie didn't really want to die, but yet he was at the point he didn't care either. He wanted sympathy and pity, but most of all, he wanted out of jail.

When his sentence was up, he was released—

but for what? I was soon to realize that this had been but my first encounter with him. During the 3 ½ years I worked there, I probably had him in and out of jail a dozen times. Each time he came he was in the same condition. I saw him through seven attempted suicides.

 The last time he came down to my office.

"My stomach is upset."

"Here are some Amphogel tablets. Take one every three to four hours."

He still stood a minute.

"They're transferring me to the State Penitentiary tomorrow."

He looked small and scared. I doubt that his stomach bothered him. I think he just wanted to tell me.

Ronnie had outgrown our facilities. I've often wondered if he ever got straightened out, realizing how limited my attempts at helping him had really been . . .

   End of this short story.

I want to relate two other papers, exactly as they were written for an English class that were based on my jail experiences.

THE LITTLE DRUNK

The most interesting type I have known at the jail is what I like to refer to as "The Little Drunk." This man or woman probably has a lifetime of experiences that most people never hear about or even care to hear about. I have met thousands of them from many different life styles.

It would be interesting to take one particular older drunk, start to follow him step by step through his life from the early childhood, through school and middle age to his present state. To find out how his childhood started out, if he had any love, care or understanding. Some of them, most likely, had normal childhoods but grew up only to find the real world to menacing to cope with. Or maybe he even obtained a decent education and became successful only to have what seemed to be insurmountable problems arising during this time.

What I have been writing is only speculation on why some lives end in drinking.

What kind of pattern does the drunk follow when he is really a total alcoholic? Some still attempt to hold successful jobs. Others end up losing their homes, belongings, plus their own respect and the respect of anyone else. Many, at this point, turn to crime as a means of support for their habit. This starts a vicious cycle of police intervention, jail terms, and paroles, only to repeat the same thing over and over again.

Can anyone really say who is the blame for this? Society is beginning to respond more to this problem as a sickness rather than a criminal intention on the drunk's part. Some cities are trying to rehabilitate these people and give them another chance at life. To rehabilitate these people requires an effort and desire on their part, cooperation from the police, and the general public in financial support.

This problem would never be totally eradicated, but I feel the country as a whole would be improved with a more concentrated effort to help fight his problem.

End of this piece.

This next piece I wrote as if I was actually an inmate in the drunk tank.

DRUNK TANK

I could feel myself lying on a hard cold floor. I attempted, groggily, to open my eyes and focus them in the dimly lit room. A wave of nausea hit me and I struggled without success to hold it. It came, bitter and foul all over my shirt and the floor I was lying on. The first wave passed and I felt somewhat relieved. I rolled over away from the smell and pulled myself up against the wall until I felt I was sitting.

I became aware that I was not alone. There were other men with me. Some were lying in grotesque positions, arms and legs sprawled in all directions. Others were sitting or standing, staring at nothing or no one in particular. One was standing over a toilet doing what I painfully realized my body called for, if I could ever make it that far across the room. Maybe later.

I knew what this place was as I had been there many times before. A "drunk" tank and the people who inhabit them do not change. I gingerly turned my head, going slowly to fight off the feelings of dizziness, toward the windows and bars facing the outer hall. I could see a trustee mopping the hallway and deputies walking past leaving tracks on a freshly clean floor. Further beyond I could see a row of inmates, all in jail garb, filing into the mess hall. If they offered that to me I'd pass on it till the next meal. I hadn't really eaten in the last few days anyway, so another didn't seem to matter.

"Thump." I jerked my head toward the sound across from me and saw a man on the floor. His body was rigid and jerking and saliva was drooling from the corners of his mouth. Several of the drunks were at the door trying to attract the attention of a guard in the hallway. Doors slid open banging with steel against steel. Two deputies came in and knelt near the stricken man. One left and returned seconds later with a girl in a white uniform. A nurse, I guess. She seemed to put something in his mouth and then motioned for the deputy to go somewhere. For about 10 minutes she stayed there, on her knees, until two men in white came in with a stretcher and took him away.

I became aware of my own body shaking and trembling. I could see her coming toward me and realized I had to talk to her. My hand reached up and I must have mumbled something as she asked two of the deputies to help me to her office.

Her office was small and seemed so white and clean. I became conscious of my clothes, dirty and torn, and the soles of my shoes flapping as they had for the past month.

I was placed in a chair and she was asking me questions.

"Do you take any routine medications on the outside?"

I nodded, but couldn't remember what kind.

"Do you have seizures?"

Again I nodded.

"How many times a day do you take them?"

I indicated three times. She was holding two different kinds out to me. My hands were shaking so bad I could not hold them. She placed them in my mouth and gave me some water.

Then she was pouring a red liquid into the glass. This was the stuff I wanted. It would let me rest a few hours and stop some of the shaking. It was bitter and my stomach wanted to expel it. I fought to keep it down and it stayed, at least for now.

She was holding my hand and asking how I had cut it. I looked and saw an angry red sore with dark blood crusted and caked with dirt. I vaguely remember it hurting several days ago and told her this.

She had a basin and was soaking away the dirt and blood. Then she applied a bandage that seemed shockingly white next to my grubby clothes.

"Have you had a tetanus shot recently?"

I shook my head and told her it had been back in 1966 that I had received my first one. I could see her fixing a needle and felt the sharp jab on my arm and then it was over.

"I'll bring some medications to your cell tonight, and then if you are here in the morning I'll have you on the sick call list to see the doctor."

Back in the drunk tank I curled up in a corner trying to shut out the others, cursing and talking and yelling.

I didn't know if I would be a kick-out in the morning or if I would be loaded on a bus and taken to see the judge. I rather hoped I would see the judge and hear him say 60–90 days in jail. I realized I depended on jail to thaw me out once in awhile, feed me and restore my body and health. I could feel sleep coming and I put all thought aside. It didn't really matter anyway, what happened to me. Let tomorrow happen as it might.

End of this story.

Just one other incident I wanted to recall was a happening outside the jail.

I went into a convenience store and was the only person in there besides the sales clerk. I saw two men come in the door and separate. One of them saw me, and I spoke to him. He was well known to me

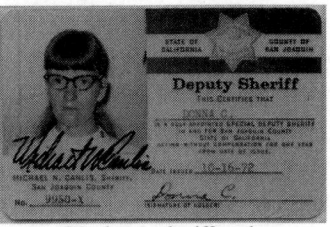
My deputy sheriff card.

from the jail. After he saw me, they both left. I think I may have stopped a robbery that day.

There are so many stories from my jail work.

It was a very hard, demanding, and a long hours-type of job. It was a very challenging and creative work.

JEEP FUN

As I mentioned in the past, Lee and I continued to explore and go to the mountains whenever we had a chance. We had the jeep and could go off roading to places completely isolated except for us. We had a tent, camping gear, and sleeping bags. One time, we set up the tent and went to sleep. The next morning, we found the whole world covered with snow.

The jeep had a winch on it, which got us out of a few messes involving snow and mud. One time Lee was in the jeep on a hill and the jeep rolled over with him in it, but he was okay. Sometimes we went on excursions with other jeeps.

One time we went camping up by a place called Semen Meadows. We set up the tent and then decided to walk up to the other end of the meadow, about a half a mile away. There were trees to our left—fairly close. We had our puppy, a poodle named Teddy, with us. He was out a little ahead of us. When we got about three-quarters of the way up the meadow, two wolves came out of the trees to our left. They were in front of us and one stayed on the left while the other circled over to the right of us. They did not growl or act hostile or threatening. They sat down on their hind quarters. We immediately picked up Teddy and turned around and started walking back toward our campsite. They never tried to follow or bother us. We figured they had a lair in the trees and were just guarding their family. That night we made a big fire and lay with one ear open. After that incident, we never went exploring or camping without a gun.

We used to run across old, abandoned towns and mills. One old house we found had shelves all over it, which held various bottles with rocks in them. There were also rocks setting loosely on the shelves. We used to find years-old magazines and newspapers. We never took any of them, just looked and enjoyed. Lee was a lot of fun to go places with, and we enjoyed those years.

After working at the jail for a few years, I started becoming interested in the law enforcement angle. I felt my military background, plus my years as a jail nurse, might help me land a job in law enforcement.

So I started a letter campaign. I sent letters to 80 some larger cities across the United States. Many never responded; however, I did get a few positive sounding responses.

The place I finally decided to move to was Davenport, Iowa.

But let me digress a bit and say that Lee and I did end up getting a divorce. I guess I felt I did not want to be the only one working the rest of my life. Also, Lee did like to spend money on all of his hobbies. If I could say anything to Lee, I would say I am more than sorry for the wrongs that I did during our marriage and still think of him fondly and wish him well. The divorce was final early in 1973. Lee returned to Ohio.

START LIFE AGAIN

I moved into an apartment in Stockton; I believe in late 1972. Lee and I had two dogs at that time. Both were toy poodles. He took Teddy and left Snicky with me.

Well, wouldn't you know it? Snicky was pregnant. So one night in the middle of the night, I woke up and she had delivered a pup in bed with me. I made a place in the bathroom, and she had several more there. One was not breathing, and I gave it mouth to nose resuscitation and rubbed its abdomen, and it started to breath.

I planned to be moving. So as soon as they were big enough, I sent two to Lee, and I sent the tiniest one to my folks in Illinois. They had never had a pet in the house. When they met the plane and picked him up, they fell in love with him right away. I had named him Button. Daddy fixed up a box and a lamp for warmth at home and soon Button was Daddy's dog. Button lived for about eleven years with them. When he died, Daddy made a coffin with a metal grave marker for him and placed him behind the house near his orchard. I know he missed Button very much.

When I gave notice at the jail that I would be leaving, they searched for a new nurse. Several came and went before this one young nurse thought she would like it. She stayed, and I trained her and moved on. I later heard that they soon had round-the-clock nurses at the jail. I can believe it, as it was a tremendous amount of work for one person.

DAVENPORT, IOWA

Now was the time to move on with my life. I moved to Davenport, Iowa. I got a small apartment from a really nice elderly couple. I had decided I was going to stop nursing forever and go into law enforcement. So I started all the paper work for the Davenport Police Department. Meanwhile, I took a job at a pancake house to make a little cash. I also started at the Muscatine Community College to obtain an Associate Degree in Law Enforcement. The classes were taught in Davenport at the police department by an instructor that came up from Muscatine several nights a week.

I was in the process at this time of going through all the various tests for the police department: the physical, the agility test, the psychological test, and others, which I have forgotten by now. It was quite a process just to get through all of that.

JIM

Soon after I started college, I started dating a guy named Jim. He just happened to be the instructor of my college classes. I felt at the time that he was intelligent, well educated, and very humorous with his students. I did not know at the time how drastically he was to change my life. All for the worse! He was absolutely the worst person I could have hooked up with. Of course, at that time I did not realize any of that or what would happen. It still angers me even to be thinking about him this many years later.

We started dating and I was soon to meet his

two sons, Jamie and Jay. They were about 10 and 8 when I first met them. Jamie was fine, but Jay had lots of emotional and some other problems that were quite serious. I was naïve, and though I did not have any experience with kids, I felt I could cope with them and with Jay's problems. I felt that my education would be of some help in coping and helping. Wrong!!! Wrong!!!

Jim asked me to marry him and I accepted. Again, I don't think Mother and Daddy were thrilled, but they rallied behind us. About the same time I said "yes" to Jim, the Davenport Police Department told me I was accepted and gave me a starting date. I was so excited. I felt my life was coming together. Instead it was starting on a fast downward spiral.

Then Jim dropped the bombshell. He said I could have one or the other. I could either marry him, or I could join the police department, but I could not do both. He said he was not going to have a wife of his running around in a cop car. I actually think he never thought the offer would happen. So this is where I totally messed up my whole life. I chose Jim and declined the police department.

We were married in the Lostant Methodist Church back home. The boys were there. After the wedding, we bought this old but beautiful house in Muscatine, Iowa, to live in. The boys lived with us part of the time and part of the time with their mother in Illinois.

Unfortunately, I was back to being a nurse. I chose a job as chief nurse of a family practice center in Muscatine. It had five doctors and was a clinic setting for each doctor. I hired staff, did all the work of a chief nurse, such as evaluations, scheduling, and numerous other jobs. I again did inventory for all five clinics and also filled in for various clinics as necessary. I was also there to field any problems that arose.

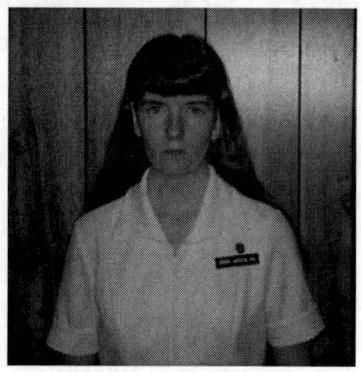
Me in my nurses uniform.

I continued going to college and earned my Associates Degree in Law Enforcement in June of 1975 at the Muscatine Community College.

At the same time, I was keeping house and semi-raising two boys because Jim was gone a lot. When he was home, we often had various students at the house for one reason or another.

I don't know when it all started, because a wife is always the last to know. I did not know it in Muscatine, but Jim had relationships with female students from his classes. He continued to get in trouble at every college where he was employed.

We had to leave Muscatine, and he got a job at a college in Minot, North Dakota. So we moved there in 1975. It was in Minot that it all came to light, and I found out about all of his sexual relations with his female students. He had several relationships there and nearly ruined one girl's life. Another girl even called me. I left Jim early in 1976 and left for California. We were not divorced, only separated.

I was devastated. I moved into an apartment and took a job at a hospital in Daly City. It was a job on an alcoholic rehabilitation unit. I did very well in the job and liked the work.

I was trying to decide what to do when Jim came out to see me. He wanted me to come back and promised everything would be better. Before he left, he bought me a puppy. I could not have a puppy where I lived, but he left it there anyway. The puppy chewed the rug and curtains because I was gone to work most of the time. I also lived on the second floor. I got an apartment full of fleas. I had exterminators and everything else, but could not get rid of them. I had to move to another place. I sent the dog to Jim.

I believe he came out again and wanted to try it again. This was the second worst mistake I made in my life. I went back. By this time, Jim had been told to leave Minot and had landed in Lebanon, Illinois. He had bought a modular home on a piece of land in Lebanon. It had several bedrooms and was not in great condition.

I did not realize any of that until I went back. By then, the kids were living with us most of the time and going to school there. We were the main parents at the time. Judy and her boyfriend had them occasionally.

I was able to attend the four-year college Jim was now teaching at for free as a spouse of a staff member. Also my VA benefits would run out if I did not use them. So I took one year and went back to school and got my Bachelor of Arts Degree in two majors. One was in Criminal Justice and the other was in Psychology. I maintained a 4.0 average and graduated in May of 1978 from McKendree College.

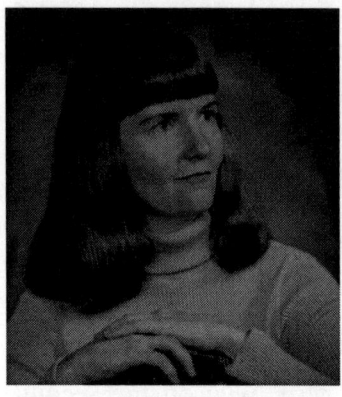
Graduation picture from McKendree College, 1978.

I was going to school full-time, raising a family, helping Jim by writing as he dictated his master's thesis, and then I typed it. I also helped him to write tests for his classes and helped to grade papers.

I never could get along with Jay and problems with him continued to escalate.

Jim never stopped having relationships with female students. I came to realize he never would.

Jim, over the 7–8 years we were married, mentally abused me until I had no feelings of self-worth. He criticized everything about me. He made me feel less than nothing. I felt afraid at times. (After I left him, it took me many years to rebuild my self-esteem.)

I cannot even think about him without anger rising inside myself. I choose not to go into any more of the multitude of problems we had. It was a disastrous marriage and practically ruined my life.

I had to get the divorce. I left everything with him except my clothes and a few household things that I could carry. In fact, the day I moved out, he was up in Muscatine, was very angry, and told me if I wasn't gone by the time he came back things would be rough. I called my folks, and they drove four hours to help me get packed and out. He kept the house and furniture and many, many guns he had bought, because he was a gun dealer too. I left with nothing. I just wanted to get away so badly. I did not ask for anything in the divorce as I never wanted to hear from him again. (Over the years I did see and hear from Jamie a few times, and I thought that was extra nice. He is a good person.)

START LIFE ALL OVER—AGAIN

This life started in Bellville, Illinois, in the late '70s to early '80s. Both times I was divorced, I was left with no money and some existing bills. For me, I had worked now for about 15 years and had nothing to show for it. All the money I had made was gone and not by my hand.

I was living in a small apartment not too far from the hospital where I was working. I was working in Bellville on a psychiatric unit. I don't really recall how long I worked in psych before an opening came up on the dialysis unit in the hospital.

When I went to nurses' training, there was no such thing as dialysis. If a patient's kidneys failed, they died. This procedure had been developed over the previous few years.

I applied for a job with this unit. The head nurse of this unit was Sister Jamesine. She accepted me and I started training. There is a lot to learn about dialysis and a lot of patient teaching to do.

As a side note, Sister Jamesine and I keep in touch and occasionally get together. We use e-mail mostly. She is truly a fantastic person and a good friend. In fact, it was her suggestion that planted the idea in my head to write down these life experiences.

Back to dialysis. The unit had seven chairs. The patients sat in recliners. These chairs could tilt all the way back if needed. Some patients came in beds if they were too sick to come any other way. Sometimes you had to take a dialysis machine to a patient's room to do the procedure.

The first dialysis machine I learned on was the old Travenol with a washtub-like affair that surrounded the artificial kidney filter. Sorry if I did not get that right as I forget a lot about this machine. The other machines in the room were more modern.

Patients usually came 2–3 times a week for anywhere from 2.5 to 5 hours a treatment. Some were on the waiting list for a transplant.

I do not plan to write a long dissertation about dialysis and all of the trials and problems that go along with it. As nurses, we got to know the patients very well, and we felt for them as they went through their lives on dialysis.

CALIFORNIA CALLING

I loved California, and it seemed to be the place I always wanted to go back to. Also at this time, my brother, John, and his wife, Linda, were living in Concord. So this was a special added feature.

I had written a few letters looking for openings in dialysis units. The hospital I wanted to go to was in San Mateo, California. They had a big dialysis unit, and it was in a very good location south of San Francisco. At the time I was moving, they did not have any openings but would keep my name for the next available opening.

So I went to Santa Rosa and worked in a free-standing dialysis unit for awhile. I had a cute, little loft apartment and a bike. I did a lot of bike riding there. Santa Rosa is about 1 ½ hours north of San Francisco and so beautiful. It is located right in the middle of wine country. I did a lot of exploring while I lived there.

Then the call came from the San Mateo hospital, and I took a job there in dialysis. I had found a niche in nursing that was very fulfilling, paid well, and was a good job for me. The year was probably about 1982. I found an apartment in San Bruno and felt like I was pretty well set up for living in California. I worked for an excellent head nurse named Darlene at this hospital. She became a friend as well.

While working dialysis, I decided to get a part-time job at the Stanford Blood Bank to earn extra money. I wanted to get enough to have a down payment on my own condo. It was 1985–86 before I was able to buy my own place. I got a one-bedroom condo at this really nice resort-like complex. There were about 1300 condos in a lot of different buildings. It had three pools, a clubhouse, and very beautiful grounds.

A BETTER LIFE—MAYBE

My main source of entertainment was going hiking with the Sierra Club. We went on different trails all around the area. It was not safe to go places like that as a single woman. Some of the hikes were fairly difficult. I also went hiking some with a girlfriend or two. I dated some but nothing serious.

I had a condo of my own, a decent car, and some savings in the bank. In addition, I was saving through a retirement plan at work that was mine to keep forever. I put as much money as I could in this plan. It started to build. So for the first time in my life, I was getting ahead.

Then I started feeling bad. I did not know I was sick yet. This was the fall of 1986. I had to stop the hiking. I was so tired, and I lacked enough energy to do it any more. I used all my energy to keep working. It went on like this until the spring of 1987.

Working in dialysis, we had to get our liver enzymes blood work drawn every two months to guard against hepatitis. One test came back indicating I had elevated liver enzymes. I was sent to a specialist who did more tests and a liver biopsy. This was very painful. There was something wrong, but they could not make a definitive diagnosis. They ruled out hepatitis B, mainly because I had received shots to prevent this when I first started at the hospital. Even though I was sick, I never had any time off from work except when I got the biopsy. They never really did anything to treat me, just followed my blood work. I gradually got better.

However, other things were breaking down at the same time. My menses stopped. They played around trying to give me hormones, which I was unable to take. I really can't remember now all the reasons why I could not take them. So I was in my early 40s when I stopped my menses cycle.

At the same time, I developed adult rosacea. It is like all of a sudden developing a bad case of acne on the face that will not go away. I saw another specialist for this. Fortunately, it could be treated, and I will continue this treatment for the rest of my life.

They decided the hepatitis was not a contagious type, and I did not have to restrict my living or work. They said some women at my age got "that," even though they didn't really know what "that" was.

I did not think a great deal more about the illness at that time after I started getting better.

TOM

At that same time, I met Tom. The year was 1987. Darlene and I had gone out to a ballet. I had dressed special, in a skirt and blouse and heels, to go with her. When I got back home, I realized that something was going on in the clubhouse. I decided, since I was already dressed up, to go down and see what was happening. There was a dance in progress. I decided to just stay a little while and watch.

I was sitting there, and Tom came up and asked me to dance. We danced several dances. It was late and I had to leave. We had not even gotten each other's last name or any information about each other.

I was to learn later that Tom had wanted to find me. He knew what kind of car I drove and the color, but had no idea where I lived or in which one of the many garages I parked. So he started going through garages after work but never could find it. That was because I worked evenings, and my car was always gone when he was looking.

A few weeks later, I had to go to the clubhouse for something, and I saw him out by the pool. I went over to say "hi," and we talked a little. He asked me if I wanted to go to the pool party that was coming up on a weekend. He said he would save me a seat and to come if I could.

I gave it a lot of thought. It had been about 6–7 years since Jim, and I had not done any real dating. I decided to do it. So I went out that day, and sure enough, he had saved me a seat. We got to know each other and started dating.

I was soon to meet his children: a girl, aged 5, and a boy, aged 8. The boy was

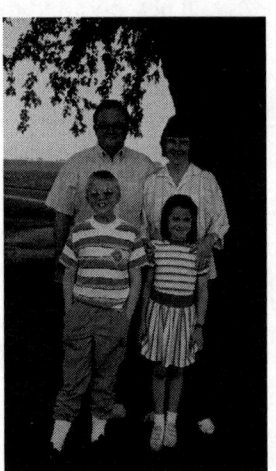

Tom and I with his children Michael and Jennie.

developmentally handicapped in a fairly severe way. He took a lot of special handling and care, and Tom was very adept at being with him.

Tom was hurting as he had just separated from his wife. He had no idea why his wife wanted a divorce. He was told to leave, and that is why he had taken an apartment in the same, huge complex I lived in.

During the first year we were dating, we took a vacation once with the kids down to Florida to meet his family. His mother and father lived in a condo in Homestead. He had three brothers living in Florida who came to meet us too.

We took the kids to Disneyworld. Being with a little girl, I saw every bathroom in the entire park. I really got along well with Jennie, and it was a good vacation. That was the first time I had met Tom's family too.

Tom's job was working for DOD (Department of Defense) as a warehouse supervisor. He had joined the civil service in 1976. While he worked in the warehouse, he was studying on his own about computers and programming. Computers were very new at this time. He wrote the program to handle the entire inventory at his warehouse. It was still being used when he left. Tom was self-taught using the computers. Tom is very intelligent and diligent when he wants to learn something.

We talked about marriage and made plans to be married down in Key Largo, Florida, in September 1988. We wanted the wedding there, as Tom's youngest brother was very sick with AIDS, and we wanted him to be at our wedding. That was not to be. Jim died before our wedding. We went to his memorial.

We did continue with the wedding plans and were married 4 Sept. 88. Tom's family and my family came down for the wedding. It was held at the Sheraton Hotel in Key Largo, and they had a wedding planner who really helped us put it all together by long distance.

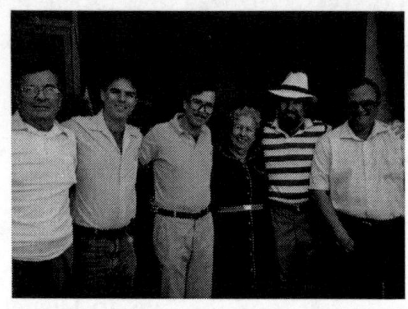

Tom's dad, Bion, Bill, Jim, Tom's mother Betty, Jack, and Tom

After the wedding, we went on our honeymoon at Sanibel Island off the west coast of Florida. That was such a beautiful and relaxing time. We found so many seashells. We both just loved it there.

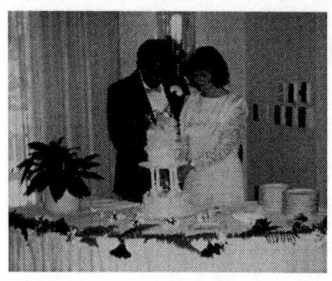

Our wedding.

Back home, we both continued to work. Tom's kids would visit and stay with us every other weekend and on other occasions. I was learning about Michael and how to deal with his limitations.

In 1989 Tom's work started plans to close the

base in Alameda. That meant that Tom could soon lose his government job.

He applied for a job as a computer specialist and obtained that, but he still needed a place to go when the base closed. So he applied for a job with DOD in Columbus, Ohio, and was accepted. The government would move our belongings. They also helped some in paying closing costs on a new home in Columbus.

We were still working and living in the Bay Area when the big '89 earthquake (7.1 on the Richter scale) hit. I was in the condo, and things flew around and fell off desks and shelves. I could see the walls and windows rolling. The floor was moving, so I had to hold on. All the lights went out, so it was dark. I headed for the door to get out of the building and found our terrarium with our collection of shells had shattered on the floor in front of the door. I had to scrape that away before I could open the door to get out. When I opened the door, the hallways were pitch black, and I had to feel my way to the closest stairwell. This was black too. Everybody else must have done the same because lots of people were standing outside.

Tom was very lucky. He had just reached our side of the Bay Bridge in his car. Part of the bridge collapsed in that earthquake.

We made it through pretty well. Our condo must have been built to earthquake standards, because we had minimal structural damage. We were concerned about our being able to sell the condo after this, but it sold at a good price.

COLUMBUS, OHIO AND DOD

We left to move to Columbus in mid-December of '89. The trip was really rough as the weather was extremely cold and snowy, especially in Nebraska. We were driving two cars across country, so each of us had to drive a full day. For three mornings straight in Nebraska, my car would not start due to the cold, and we had to call AAA. It was 20 below all that time.

Tom was to report to his new job on the 26th of December. We stayed in government housing the first couple of months while looking for a house.

We discussed my work and decided this would be a good time for me to stop nursing if I wanted too. I wanted to get a civil service job, but there weren't any openings at this time.

I worked temporarily at Penny's department store for a few months. Then I finally took a nurse's job in a psych clinic. During this time, I was taking clerical and other tests required for a government job. I passed these. Finally, I got the phone call and was hired over the phone.

The job was in accounts payable for DOD. I reported for duty on 12 Nov 91. We had a six-week orientation course. Boy, it was difficult—so much to learn about paying bills for governmental contracts. I had never done anything except nursing and had no idea if I could do that or not, but I learned and excelled. I worked hard at that job for nine years.

One person I want to mention is my friend Vicki. She started a few months after me. I was instrumental in helping her learn about the section where we worked. We ended up working together all nine years. We still are friends and communicate by e-mail fairly often.

I want to back up a year to 1990. I had tried to get a life insurance policy, and they took blood work. I got a report denying me any life insurance and suggesting I contact a doctor for elevated liver enzymes. I was referred to a specialist, and he did another liver biopsy. In fact, he did two because the first time he missed. The end result was that he could not give me a definitive diagnosis but agreed to follow me.

In Dec. of '92, Tom's father passed away. He had been sick for a number of years. Tom's father was a veteran and had been an air traffic controller. This was very hard on Betty, his wife, to have first lost a son and then her husband.

The end of '92 and the first three months of '93, I became very ill. My whole body turned yellow, every part of me. My urine was the color of a dark coffee. I saw my doctor and had my third liver biopsy and lots more blood work. I was extremely sick then.

The doctor said there were two choices. If he gave me the medications he thought were necessary, I would either start getting better or I would get much worse. He still had not made a diagnosis and said he could not make the decision. He referred me to Dr. Robert Kirkpatrick at Ohio State University Hospital. I went to see him, and he got all my files and lab work and biopsy reports. He called me at home and said I had to start medication that day. He called in a prescription for Prednisone and Imuran. The Prednisone was started at a high dose and gradually tapered down. He was able to immediately diagnose my condition. It was Auto Immune Chronic Active Hepatitis. Finally, I at least knew what I was dealing with. The medication immediately started to work. I felt better.

I will be on these medications all of my life. I started the medications in Feb. of '93. I have been on them, in varying dosages, depending on current lab work, for over 12 years now. All of these years, I have also had to have my blood work checked frequently. It started off every few weeks, then it went to every month, and then to every two months. Currently, I am on every three months. I also have to continue to see the doctor periodically.

DADDY

During the time I was so very sick, in Feb. of '93, I insisted we take a trip to Illinois to see my parents. Maybe I did not know if I would get better. I don't remember now. I was very yellow and feeling really terrible. I remember before we left that I told Daddy that I loved him. That was not something we said every day to each other. June and Phil were also visiting at the same time, so I got to see them too.

I was always so glad we made that trip, because it was the last time I ever saw my father alive.

In May of 1993, the same year, Mother and Daddy were on vacation at my brother John and Linda's place in California.

We got a call that Daddy had had a severe brain stem stroke. It happened at breakfast time, right in their house. He was taken to the hospital by ambulance and put on a life support system. This was done only to allow all his family to get to California. June came from Michigan, Robert came from Dayton, Ohio, and I came from Columbus.

I remember sitting by Daddy's beside and holding Daddy's hand and bending over because my stomach hurt so much. My medicine was starting to cause an ulcer. The stress of this situation probably aggravated it.

The whole family and mother went back to Illinois for the funeral. Daddy was a Mason and the Masonic Lodge performed the Masonic rites at the funeral. This was such a very hard time for the whole family. We had lost the first one of our immediate family. Daddy was buried in the Lostant Cemetery next to Mother's parents.

LIFE GOES ON

Life has to go on, and we went back to work and living. I saw the doctor and was started on Axiam, which was to heal my stomach and prevent ulcers. I had to stay on this for years. Later on, it caused me severe headaches, and I had to switch to Prilosec and even later switched to Nexium—another medication to take the rest of my life.

In the mid-ninties, I started having more problems in a different way. I became very hyper, irritable, had a racing pulse, and many other symptoms. I was found to have hyper-thyroid syndrome. I saw another specialist and had radiation to kill the thyroid. I was told to return in a certain time for reevaluation. Long before that time came, I became slow and sluggish, and my skin started to slough. My hands had skin flaking all over. I could not speak properly nor think clearly. I went back to the doctor early, and he was surprised. He said he had never seen a person go hypo-thyroid so quickly. He started me on thyroid medication, which also will be taken for the rest of my life.

I never did have any time off from work through all these illnesses. I kept going, although I should not have.

All these years, since we left California, we would have Jennie and Michael fly out to visit us every year. Sometimes they came together, sometimes separately. Tom so looked forward to seeing them. He really missed his kids. I believe that was the hardest part of moving for him.

Somewhere in the mid-nineties, Michael went to live at a Camphill Community in New York called Triform. This was a place for special needs young adults to live in a group setting, hopefully to learn a craft and the skills necessary to live on their own some day.

We went to visit him several times while he was there. The setting was a farm with about five houses, a barn, large gardens, and fields. It had animals, such as cows, sheep, pigs, and chickens. Each house had house parents and a number of residents like Michael.

Michael had been at this community for 4–5 years when he decided he did not want to return. He stayed in California.

HEART TROUBLE COMING

In 1995, Tom was at work and started to have chest pains. (He was about 52.) He went to the dispensary on post and was transferred by ambulance to the hospital. They called me at my job, and I met him at the hospital. He was admitted for overnight observation. I left at the end of visiting hours and went home to bed. We always sleep with a fan on and do not hear the phone. So all of a sudden, there was someone at the door. It was the police. They said the hospital was requesting that I return right away. I returned and found that he had had a massive heart attack around 10:30 that night. If he had not been at the hospital and on the cardiac monitor, he might not have survived.

The next day they sent him, via ambulance, to another hospital across town that could do angioplasty. He had a balloon procedure done during angioplasty. Tom was home for a while after that, recovering.

Right after Tom got home from the hospital,

his brother, Jack, came up to stay a week with him so I could go back to work. That was so nice and was so mind relieving to know that he was with Tom.

One major thing affected me a lot. From that time on, I had to do all the snow shoveling, snow blowing, and snow removal. We had a snow blower, but there was always shoveling to be done too. Some years we had such big storms and so many that I could not keep up with our small blower. One year we had to dig a tunnel through the snow to get the car out. I always had to shovel the steps and the entry way to the driveway, especially after the street plow came through and filled it up with hard slush and ice. I had to shovel the deck so the puppy could get out the doggy door. I also shoveled a path out into the yard so she had a place to go. Sometimes all the shoveling and blowing had to done several times a day if the snow continued coming down.

In the summer, I did most of the mowing of the grass, which is hard work too. I did a lot of raking of leaves and other yard work.

Tom's heart condition really changed our lives. We always lived with the concern—could it happen again?

At this same time, Tom developed diabetes and had to be concerned about his diet, not only for the heart problem, but also for the diabetes. He was placed on oral medications for both. It was one more thing he had to deal with.

Tom had been diagnosed, in the early '90s, with a disease called Mitochondrial Myopathy. This is a condition that involves every cell in the body. It was diagnosed by a biopsy taken from his upper arm muscle. He is on medication that he takes every day just to hold it at bay.

MY MOTHER

I have mentioned previously that my folks were living on an 80-acre farm in Illinois that had once belonged to my mother's father's side of the family. When Daddy died in '93, Mother continued to live on the farm alone. She lived about 5 miles from the Lostant Methodist Church and her best friend, Dolores. She was about 15 miles from LaSalle-Peru, good for getting groceries, doing shopping, and seeing her doctors. When Daddy died, Mother was 83. Mother was always a survivor. She was always able to make do and take care of things, even after Daddy's death.

But some things even she could not fight. She was developing macular degeneration. Her eyesight would continue to get worse.

For a few years, Mother spent her winter months with her children. She would live in each of our homes for part of the time. This gave mother and us a chance to visit and helped to ensure her safety during the rough weather.

In her late 80s, she was told by her doctor that she could no longer drive. It was not safe for her or for anyone else on the road. Dolores helped out by taking her shopping and to the doctor's appointments, while mother explored what her next step in life would involve.

Each one of her children looked around in their area for a retirement home that would offer independent living and be able to offer dependent living or nursing care if that time arose. Mother looked at each place that we found, but really fell in love with a place called Trinity in Beavercreek, Ohio. Another plus was that Robert, my youngest brother, lived only about 10 minutes away.

Months of preparation were already going into this move. Mother wanted all of her keepsakes and treasures to be divided up among the four kids at that point, while she was alert and aware of what she was doing. Mother never denied that at some point in the future she might not stay as aware as she was right then. Mother always dealt with reality.

All four of us met at her house one weekend and equitably made these divisions.

Also, mother had to decide on parting with a lot of her big furniture as she could take only a few of her favorite items with her. The furniture was also divided and the remaining was sent to an auction barn for sale.

My sister, June, and Robert were very instrumental in helping Mother deal with so many of the details and in actually moving her to Trinity. They also helped her get settled in there.

Mother loved Trinity and fit in there beautifully. She made friends and took part in the activities. She took crochet lessons and learned how to crochet at about 90–91 years of age. She continued to crochet even while her eyesight was getting worse. She never thought small. The first thing she crocheted was a bedspread of all different colors for her bed. She taught me the fundamentals of crocheting, and I still enjoy crocheting.

Mother used the exercise room and went on walks on the beautiful paths on the grounds outside Trinity. She loved to watch the Canadian geese on these walks or from her window. She always wanted to stay in shape as best she could. She did all this using her walker, as she was unsteady without it.

Mother attended the church service given at Trinity every Sunday. She attended ice cream socials and various performances given at Trinity.

Mother also loved their Christmas tree and decorations and other seasonal decorations. They also had a big bird cage with small birds and nests that were relaxing to look at.

Each one of us children would have Mother come and stay in our homes for a while each year. We all also came and visited with her at Trinity quite often.

Tom and I came every month to visit while we were living in Columbus. We would take her shopping and out to eat. Usually, we went to Bob Evan's Restaurant, as that was her favorite place. In all the years past, when Mother and I would get together, we would make it a practice to go out for a hot fudge sundae. She loved this and looked forward to it. So we did that off and on when we came to see her.

Mother loved all of the visits. She had visits from Dolores and also from a few other friends from out of town too. In the later years, she might not have remembered the visits, but at the time, she loved them.

One time we were down for a visit and mother fell, even though she had her walker, and we were right beside her. She really had a bad fracture of her right wrist. I can still picture her sitting on the floor cradling her arm next to her body while we waited for the nurses. She had to go to the hospital for a cast. I stayed in her room at Trinity with her for a few days until she was able to deal with it. Even that never stopped her. The staff gave her physical and occupational therapy and helped her to learn how to dress with one arm and hand. Nothing was easy, but mother went through it all okay. Her wrist and hand were okay when the cast came off. I felt so bad that she had to have that extra burden.

Mother loved to read and always read a newspaper or books and the Bible. She did this until her vision became so bad that she had to stop. She never did like TV, probably because she could not hear it well. She wore hearing aids, but was still quite deaf even with them on.

Ever since Daddy died in 1993, I made it a practice to call mother two times a week. I continued this practice at Trinity. She loved these calls, even when she got so forgetful she could not really remember them. Each call was new and good. The other kids called too, and she loved to get all the news. Mother truly loved her kids and their extended families.

Mother started becoming increasingly forgetful in her later years. She was aware of it too, and I am sure that it bothered her.

I will stop here with Mother's story and pick it up again a little later in this writing.

HEART TROUBLE—AGAIN

I mentioned a lot about Tom's heart attack in 1995 already. Now in 1999, Tom developed further problems.

He was again at work and started having chest pains. He was seen by the nurse and doctor at the DOD dispensary. He was given nitro and taken right away to the hospital. Again, I was notified and met him at the hospital.

The next morning he was transferred via ambulance to the hospital across town where he could receive the angioplasty. They did that right away. We were told that there was not any choice. Tom needed a four-way bypass open heart surgery. We both cried. We both had dreaded thinking about this surgery.

He had the surgery and developed a few arrhythmias that kept him a day or so longer in the hospital. They still only kept him in 4–5 days before they discharged him. I was so surprised when John, my brother, showed up before surgery and stayed with me for a few days to help me get through it. I thank him for that.

We were both scared of what going home meant. He could not get to the bathroom at first by himself. I bought a plastic stool to set in the shower so he could take a shower.

Again, one of Tom's brothers, Bill, came to stay with him that first week, because I had to go back to work. That was tremendously appreciated by both of us. We appreciated both of his brothers' help during times of need.

Tom spent a long time recuperating before he went back to work.

THINKING ABOUT RETIREMENT

Tom had 30 years with DOD in October 2000.

The bypass surgery and the increase in heart problems started us thinking more about retirement and where we wanted to retire. Tom could no longer handle the cold, so staying in Ohio was not really a good option.

Before Tom's father had passed away, we had bought a condo from them in Homestead, Florida. Tom's father and mother had bought another condo in Homestead. This was great until Hurricane Andrew. His parents survived the hurricane in their condo with the roof being torn off over their heads. They had hidden in the small laundry area. Ultimately, they had to move out and rebuild their condo.

Our condo was completely blown away. We had been renting it and were so grateful the renter and her child had the foresight to get away before that happened. She had evacuated when they had been warned to do so.

We did make a trip down to Florida to see the damage and were awed by the amount of damage all over that part of the state. By that time, there were huge mountains of rubble that had been bulldozed together. Whole areas were gone.

Our insurance company rebuilt the condo. We still could not sell it for any gain.

After that option was gone, but before the bypass surgery, we had been looking to retire in a place in central Florida. It was as far away from hurricanes as you could get. We even had money down on a place until Tom had his surgery. After the surgery, Tom could not breathe well in high humidity, so that pretty much cancelled Florida all together.

We took a vacation to Arizona and looked at Del Webb Retirement Communities in Tucson and in Phoenix. We decided against Phoenix, as the price was higher for the same home, and we did not want all the heavy traffic and freeways to deal with on a daily basis.

That is how we ended up in Tucson. We started having the home built for us while we were getting ready for both of us to retire from DOD. I retired in September of 2000, and Tom retired in October of 2000.

RETIREMENT

We were headed full tilt toward retirement. I retired, but I only had 12 years and 7 months towards retirement. This was DOD plus my military time. I was to receive only a tiny monthly pension, but anything was better than nothing.

Tom retired in October. We were able to get an estimate of his pension, but it never included what portion his ex-wife (Renee) would take. Tom could never seem to get a final answer. So we did not know how much we actually would have to live on in retirement.

We were able to sell our house in Ohio. We purchased our new home in Tucson in September of 2000. It had the usual mortgage on it.

The new house is located in a small community called Sunflower, which is north of Tucson in Marana. Sunflower has beautiful walking paths, desert landscaping, beautiful green lawns in the clubhouse area, a very nice clubhouse, an outdoor pool, and a Jacuzzi. It has a very big exercise room with lots of machines and weights. They offer tennis, pool, bocce ball, and horseshoes. They have a recreation director that offers many bus excursions and various other trips and exciting things to do. They also have numerous types of interest groups.

Tucson itself is surrounded by mountains and national and state parks with numerous hiking trails for all energy levels. The first five months we lived in Tucson, we had fun. We went hiking in all the state and national parks around our area. Tom did okay then, and we enjoyed being with each other and out in nature.

We always wanted to travel when we retired and did not really think things out very well. We bought a small travel trailer that had tent pop-outs on either end. We took a month and traveled back across the U.S., stopping to see my mother and going to the homes of each of my siblings. It was a wonderful trip lasting about 4–5 weeks. We really had fun and saw a lot together. We both loved the trip.

When we got back, reality set in. We realized we could not survive on our pensions by any means. We were way to far from social security age. Technically, we should not have retired when we did. We both had good paying jobs with DOD and good benefits, but I think I can understand that Tom was concerned about having some quality of life with his heart problems. We sold the travel trailer, because it would not be used, and it cost too much to store it.

That left us no choice but to consider work again. Jobs are not that easy to come by at our age, and in Tucson, the pay scale is also very low. We saw an ad in the paper for doing security work at the rodeo that comes here every year. We thought that might be fun. We had never seen a rodeo.

We applied with the company doing the hiring (Central Alarm). We worked the late hours and froze to death. We had no idea that it got so cold here, but let me tell you it does. We still never saw the rodeo. We were stationed to guard the cattle pens and horse pens for part of the nights. The rest of the nights we guarded the concessions stands.

At the end of the rodeo we were asked to continue working for Central Alarm. They paid $6.50 or sometimes $7.00 an hour, depending on the place you were sent. No benefits or paid time off was given.

We did this for several years and were sent to all kinds of places to work. Some were construction sites and others were companies requesting security.

Most of the time, I worked the evening shift, and Tom worked the night shift. We quickly learned about the desert wildlife, which I will describe in more detail later.

During these few years, Tom was in and out of the hospital for heart problems. He had been taking medicine for years, but it got to where it was not helping enough. Finally, in the spring of 2003, Tom had a severe increase in chest pain and possibly even had another heart attack. They alluded to it, but never decided for sure. He went into the hospital again to have a stent put in. In the past eight years, Tom had a massive heart attack, quadruple bypass surgery, seven cardiac catheterizations, several balloon procedures, and now the stent. The stent probably helped, but Tom kept having more angina, to the point where he could no longer work. He had angina even walking around the house, so Tom was off work for a year. He was not able to fly for some time during all of this.

In the fall of 2003, the doctor wanted to try a new procedure called EECP (external enhanced cardio pulsation). He said this was the only thing he had to offer Tom. He had to take 35 treatments for an hour each treatment. He could not stop them once he started them. So for one hour, five days a week, for seven weeks, Tom had these treatments. They were supposed to build collateral blood vessels to the heart muscle, thus relieving the angina. It gradually started helping, and by the time he was done and after a few more months, he was able to consider working security again.

In November of 2002, I had to leave Central Alarm because the salary just was not enough to live on. I liked the boss and the job, but I had to consider our welfare first. So I applied for a security job at the Raytheon Missile Systems on the south side of Tucson. I was accepted and am still working there and plan to continue.

It was a big job to learn, but once I learned it all, I felt good about it. It is a much better salary, and I also receive benefits. I get a lot of exercise, as there is a lot of walking to do. The hardest part is doing the 12-hour shifts. I asked for the night shift, which is 6 p.m. to 6 a.m. The people working on this shift are a close-knit group, thus you know that they will be there for you in any situation. I have a special friend named Cindy who works with me. She helps to make sure I know everything that is going on. She is a special friend, and I can talk to her about anything. We talk at work and via e-mail. I plan to work about five years or maybe more. I am 61 now, so I have been working here now for over two years. I do enjoy the work.

Once he began to feel better, Tom started looking around for a security job. He found a job working for a company called Akal Security. He is working the night shift from midnight to 8 a.m. He still has occasional angina, but is learning how to pace himself. It seems to come more in the humidity during the monsoon season. He still takes a long-acting nitro every day and carries the regular nitro for emergencies. Tom also gets exercise on this job, which is good for him. He was assigned to the Tucson Convention Center and loved it because of the great variety of events going on there. He plans to work as long as he is able. We take our health as it comes.

I want to update the news concerning Tom's illness since I wrote the past paragraph. In February and March of 2005, Tom had two more cardiac catheters with the result of three more stents being placed. He continued to have a lot of angina even after these surgeries. His boss at Akal allowed him to change his place of work and his hours to a less stressful job and time. He may have to also further decrease the number of hours worked due to continuing angina. Tom is taking another three months of cardiac rehabilitation and is also taking another 35 series of EECP treatments at this time. We hope this will help.

I wanted to briefly address my illness that is with me for the rest of my life. About 1 ½ years after we came to Arizona, I had to increase my medication to double what I had been taking in Ohio. I have to get blood work done and see the doctor periodically. I am holding my own. I am thankful that my health has been as good as it has been. Again, we take it as it comes.

MY MOTHER—AGAIN

I wanted to write about what has been happening with mother during the time we have lived in Arizona. She was the one person it was so hard to leave. Though I think as she became more forgetful she did not realize at times the length of time that passed between visits.

She continued to live at Trinity and to do very well. The four of us kids discussed whether it would be safe for her to fly out here to Arizona for a visit. She was doing well and really wanted to come. So with June and Robert on one end getting her all set up to fly and us at this end, she made the trip at the age of 91. She did fine on the airplane.

We had a very enjoyable week here, and I will treasure that memory forever. She loved seeing the desert, the cactus, and the flowers. She truly loved coming out. We went out to eat a few times, which she always loved. She made the plane ride back okay. She settled back into the routine at Trinity. It was good that she had come then, because that was the last major trip she was to make.

In December of 2002, I was still in orientation at Raytheon when I got a call from June. Mother was in the hospital for a bowel obstruction and due to have surgery. They did not know if she would survive the surgery. I flew back immediately. I stayed about a week with Mother and the family at the hospital. She had an ileostomy put in and a very serious, large abdominal incision.

When Mother was able to leave the hospital, she returned to Trinity, but after several successive hospitalizations, she was sent to Bellbrook Rehabilitation Center in Bellbrook, Ohio, because she needed a facility that could provide round-the-clock respiratory therapy. There they worked with her to try to get her active again.

Tom and I went home in March of 2003 to visit with Mother at Bellbrook Rehab. Hospital. The staff was diligent in helping her with speech therapy, occupational therapy, physical therapy, and in her learning to eat again. She was unable to do much of what they asked of her.

Mother was never the same after surgery. She was more confused and more forgetful then ever before. She did learn to eat by herself and even to push her wheelchair around with her feet, but she never was able to walk again or to take care of herself. And of course, she was never able to care for the ileostomy, so she had to remain at Bellbrook. At first, the family hired sitters at night because this seemed to be the time she was the most confused. We were concerned that she would try to get out of bed and fall and hurt herself. She also had several return trips to the hospital during this time for various reasons. She had a continuous foley catheter, so she had recurring urinary tract infections, some of which required hospital intervention.

Then in September 2003, when mother was 92, I got a call that Mother was in the hospital again. The cancer of the bowel had returned and spread, and there was nothing they could do. They said Mother would have a few lucid days to talk to the family, and then she would gradually go into a coma state until she passed on.

When I got the call, Mother got on the line

very distraught, but very aware of what was happening. She said she was dying and that she needed her kids now.

I got on a plane that evening and got into the Columbus, Ohio, airport on Saturday between 6–7 a.m. Tom was unable to come or to fly, because he was taking that series of treatments. I rented a car and drove down to Dayton and right to the hospital.

Mother was alert. The whole family was there except John and Linda from California, who were still on their way. Some of Mother's grandchildren and great-grand children were there too.

Mother was more lucid that day then she had been in a long time. She was able to talk with all of us and rested in between. We believe that day was a gift from God for all of the family and for her.

The next day (Sunday), the hospital transported mother to a hospice in Dayton. They felt she and her family could have more private and quality time together. The Hospice at Dayton was wonderful in the care they gave to her and to us. The whole family was with her for about a week and a half. Tammy, her granddaughter, came from California too. Mother passed away on 9–25–03.

The following is an exact copy of the letter I wrote to friends and family after Mother died.

I sat with mother a long time in the hospital and really felt the presence of God and felt that he was performing a miracle even during death. I know that mother felt His presence and it was evident in a number of ways.

On September 12, I received a call from my sister that mother was in the hospital and not expected to live. The doctor had told them that she would only have a few days in which she might be able to converse with family. I was able to be on the phone with mother for a few minutes but she could not hear me. She said that she needed her children and she needed them now. She said that she was dying and that God was with her. I was so touched by these statements. They will be a treasure to remember.

Tom made an airline reservation and hotel reservations and I was able to fly out that night. I got into Columbus at 0600 and rented a car to drive to Dayton. I arrived at the hospital around 0830–0900 Saturday A.M. That day was a direct gift from God to the family. Mother was completely awake and lucid and able to converse with all the family members. There was no sign of confusion that had been so prevalent the past months. John and Linda arrived from California that eve. June and Phil and Robert were already there. As were June's two sons and their families. The doctor talked with the family and with mother at the same time about dying and about what to expect in the next few days to a week. Mother was accepting and understanding and dealt well with all the doctor had to say. The family had been staying with mother 24/7 and planned to continue being with her until the end.

Sunday mother was more tired but still able to converse with the family. She was transferred to the Hospice of Dayton on Sunday night about 8 P.M. We set up plans to continue the 24/7. I volunteered to stay with her on the night shift. On Sunday and Monday night I was able to talk with mother some. We had some very meaningful moments. Mother talked about relatives who had gone before her, such as her husband and her mother. She talked about memories and about dying. I found the nights to be so serene and pleasant to be with her. I cried some every night and one time mother woke up and said it was ok—not to cry.

Mother would sometimes raise her arms up in the air from the bed. I thought she wanted a hug so I hugged her and she held me so tight. Later one of the nurses was telling me that about 80% of the patients will do that. That they are reaching out to people that have gone before. That they see these people and are tentatively looking toward heaven. That same nurse told me a story of a friend of hers who had a 22 year old son die. He would do that and one time asked the family to leave the room as there was not enough room for all the angels in the room.

I sat with mother at the hospice for 12 nights. After those first three nights the remainder of the 9 nights mother was not able to respond to us. She responded only to pain and discomfort such as when they turned her. But that was just with a moaning.

They kept her as comfortable as possible with the pain mediation which was given often. The hospice surroundings were very beautiful and serene and quiet. The hospice staff was so supportive both of mother and to the family. They talked to us about what to expect and helped us through it. Even when mother was not able to communicate with me I felt such a sense of peace being there with her. Like this was the one last thing I could offer her.

Mother passed away on Thursday 9-25-03. That was 10 years and 4 months after Daddy had died. She was 92 years old. She died at 0425. I was honored to be with her when she died.

We had a wake at Mueller Funeral Home in Lostant, Illinois. The Eastern Star (which Mother and Daddy belonged to for many years) performed a service at the wake. The funeral was held at the Lostant United Methodist Church on Monday 9-29-03.

End of this letter.

Mother was buried right next to Daddy. There were so many family and friends from the community that were there.

Mother's death has been so hard to accept and to deal with for me. It is many months now, and it seems like yesterday we were talking. I am happy she and Daddy are finally together again. I know the Lord was waiting for both of them at their own time, as He will be waiting for me when it is my time. We will be together again in Heaven.

BUSINESS

Tom always wanted to own his own business, whether it was small or big. He always felt a craving for the independence of not having to work for someone else. The first business we tried to start was when we were living in California in 1988–89.

Tom had a fair amount of computer knowledge. We started a business called "Merriam's Computing." We sold computer books and computer software at various computer shows and fairs in the San Francisco, CA, area.

Not having the capital some of the larger companies had turned out to be our biggest problem. Therefore, we could not purchase the inventory as low as they could, nor could we sell it as low as they could.

We were never really able to get it off the ground, though we worked hard at it, even while we were both working full-time at our regular jobs.

The next business Tom started by himself after our retirement in Tucson. He was in a place where he wanted to do his own thing, so he started this business without my being aware. I think he also was concerned about his health and whether he would be able to continue working. He saw this as a way to be able to earn money at home.

Tom had become interested in ham radio since we came here and thought it would be a good business to sell ham books and software on the Internet. He set up his own web site and obtained a large amount of inventory and put it all up on the Internet for sale. He bought a large amount of packing material, and we put all the inventory and packing material in our spare room. He also bought a laptop computer to work from. He refurnished our den to accommodate two desks and two computer setups. He had to have various scales and many other things to run this company. He put a top on his pickup truck and lined it with carpet so he could carry inventory in the truck safely. The name of the business is USH-AMS, Inc.

Evidently the market was not there, as he had very few sales. The only time we really sold any amount of inventory was at a ham fair held near Tucson. We both went down on a Saturday and set up and sold items at a discounted price.

Part of Tom's problem was that he was doing most of this in the year he was off work and did not have the energy or stamina to deal with everything. For a while he was just trying to move inventory by selling some on eBay, though this avenue was not profitable. It also takes time in getting the products and pictures up on eBay. He was selling at very discounted prices. Unfortunately, some of the inventory was becoming outdated and was probably a lost cause.

This business generated a lot of expenses, not offset by sales. I figure it has used $50,000 or more by this time. It has been in operation over two years now. We are currently in the process of closing the business. We donated the remainder of the inventory to the Ham Radio Club in Tucson.

When we retired, we had some retirement principal set aside that we were not planning to touch until we were able to draw social security at age 66. Then we planned to supplement social security by drawing off the interest, while leaving the principal intact.

Well, it was a good plan that did not work out. We lost some of it through the 9-11-2001 World Trade Center disaster, when stocks dropped and did not recover. We also used a lot in living expenses here in Arizona. A lot was spent that may not have needed to be spent, but it is gone, and there is nothing that can be done about it now. About three-fourths of our principal is gone.

So that leaves us working until social security at age 66 and maybe beyond. I guess it all depends upon our health.

It is sad that the business never worked out for Tom, as he devoted many hours trying to set it up and get it going. It was Tom's dream that someday we could live on the business income and neither of us would have to work again. That will probably never be the case.

PLACES I HAVE LIVED

I just wanted to make a list of the places I have lived. I have already mentioned them in my writings. I have spent 40 years working and have moved many times as this list shows. The number to the right side is the number of moves within that city. I figure all together I have moved about 30 times in my life. That many moves, as you have seen, makes for a full and interesting life. Starting out first with Illinois as the childhood home, please review as follows:

Lostant, Illinois	1st home
Lostant, Illinois	1 move
Chicago, Illinois	2 moves
San Antonio, Texas	1 move
Denver, Colorado	1 move
Heidelberg, Germany	1 move
Mannheim, Germany	1 move
Fort Hood, Texas	1 move
Killeen, Texas	1 move
Blacklick, Ohio	1 move
Columbus, Ohio	1 move
Akron, Ohio	1 move
Stockton, California	3 moves
Davenport, Iowa	1 move
Muscatine, Iowa	2 moves
Minot, North Dakota	1 move
Daly City, California	2 moves
Lebanon, Illinois	1 move
Bellville, Illinois	1 move
Santa Rosa, California	1 move
San Bruno, California	2 moves
Columbus, Ohio	1 move
Reynoldsburg, Ohio	2 moves
Tucson, Arizona	1 move

I guess that is a lot of moves in one lifetime. No wonder no one could ever keep my addresses straight. However, it does show one thing: I was able to move anywhere I wanted and immediately get a nursing job, until I decided to get out of nursing in Reynoldsburg during the last couple moves of my lifetime. This house in Tucson is the last place I intend to live unless very old age says differently.

ANIMALS AND PETS IN ADULTHOOD

I want to take time to write about animals and pets in my adult life as they have always been such a part of my entire life. I have already written about some of them so will only mention the ones that I have not talked about so far.

CORKY—When I was living in Lebanon, Illinois, I rescued a baby robin from a German Shepard. I brought her inside and set up a box for her and fed her round-the-clock, every 2–4 hours, even throughout the night until she was big enough to start eating on her own. I even came home from classes at college to feed this bird. I fed her bread soaked in milk at first, then added bits of meat. When I realized she was a real fighter and would survive, I got a fair-sized cage to keep her in.

Corky grew, and when she got old enough, I did try to release her to the wild, but she would just fly and sit on the ground or fly and sit on a branch and want to come back. I tried this several times. After that, I kept her with me. Corky's diet consisted of tomatoes, lettuce, bread, any kind of meat, and any kind of fruit. She also ate table scraps. She loved everything. She got so that if she heard the refrigerator door open she would hop around the cage expecting a treat of meat. She loved hamburgers and hot dogs. She ate most anything we had and always wanted some of it.

At the same time we had a poodle named Teddy. (This is another Teddy). Now Teddy knew if Corky did not finish all of her meat or hotdog, and he would stand trying to look in the cage until we went and got the piece and gave it to him. Teddy never tried to harm Corky or bother her otherwise.

Sometimes in the good weather, I would take the cage outside and set it in the grass or hang it from a tree. Corky loved these excursions. Other wild birds would come and land on her cage and visit her.

Inside I used to have to line the walls on two sides with plastic as Corky sure could throw the food around. I had a fair-sized area for her cage to sit in.

When she was young, I would place a dish of water in her cage, and she would take a bath. She would flutter all around in it and then sit up on a perch and preen herself. As she grew older she was less inclined to bathe, so I would sit the cage under the shower and turn it on. She always seemed to enjoy it and fluttered around and preened.

When I left Lebanon, of course, I took Corky with me to Bellville to live. When I moved to California, I took her with me there. I even took her with me on vacation or to visit relatives.

I remember when I moved to California. The trip was during the hot weather. I did not have air conditioning in the car, plus I took the southern route. I had to keep the car moving and the windows open for her all the time to keep an airflow going. I stopped for gas and motel only. I took her in the motel rooms at night with me. I was afraid I might get caught at the border going into California, but that did not happen. Corky adjusted to a California lifestyle just fine.

By the way, Corky got her name because when she was little she would bounce all over the box and looked like a cork on a fishing line going up and down.

I had Corky for 10 years and 7 months. As she got older, she lost the feathers on top of her head. I really think it was due to age. I expect she was the oldest robin ever.

Finally, shortly before one Christmas, Corky died. I was quite heartbroken as I really loved her, and she had been through a lot with me. She was always happy to see me come home after work. She would jump around her cage and want a treat. We had this routine until the very end. I took her over to my brother's home in Concord to bury her. I placed her in a small box lined with soft tissue and put in some bread. We dug a small hole under their back steps, out of the rain and weather.

PENNY—is a West Highland white terrier. Her full name is Princess Penelope as she is registered with the AKA.

Tom and I bought Penny when we lived in Columbus, Ohio, in 1991. Her birthday is March 6, 1991. Tom had never had a dog since he was a child, so this was a new experience for him. We got Penny as a tiny puppy and loved her from the beginning. She was very smart and playful.

She housebroke easily, and when we installed a doggy door, she just loved it. We always had a fenced in backyard so she could go out anytime. Back in Columbus, she would chase any rabbit or mouse or bird in the backyard. The only problem was that sometimes she caught one.

One time I came home from work to find a dead bird on the bed. Another time I came home from work to find Penny in a side room pawing and running around this small chest. I could not imagine what was going on. I pulled it out from the wall, and there was a very frightened baby bunny. Penny must have brought it in through her doggy door and then lost hold on it. Much to Penny's dismay, I took the bunny out and turned it loose, away from her backyard. The bunny was not hurt, so it must have hidden quickly after it got away inside the house.

From the time Penny was a baby, we took her on two walks a day. Finally, this was decreased to one walk a day. We always went regardless of rain or snow. Sometimes we would walk in the neighborhood, but usually we took her to the park about a mile away from our house when we lived in Reynoldsburg. Penny loved the walks and was sure to remind us if we were running late. She still does.

Penny came with us out here to Tucson and has her doggy door. She is over 14 years old now and does not move as fast as she used too. She has arthritis in her hind quarters, has lost a lot of her hearing, and does not see quite as well as she used too.

We have beautiful grounds up at the clubhouse with real grass, which Penny loves. At first, she was disconcerted by our yard here, which is all rock. Back in Reynoldsburg, she had luscious green grass in the backyard to play in, but Penny is very adaptable and got used to it. Since she is getting older, she sleeps a lot more, but she is still playful at times and still just as cute and loving as ever.

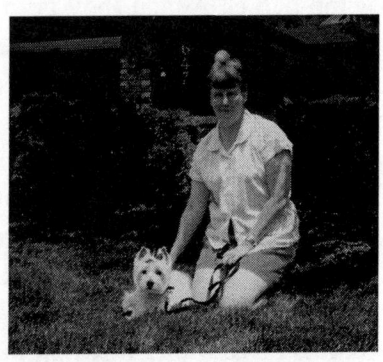

Penny and I in front of our house in the mid 90's.

She is really Daddy's little girl. Tom loves her and she him. Tom learned how to bathe her and to clip her hair. She is so relaxed when he is working on her. She will let him do anything with her. She trusts him completely.

We both love Penny and will miss her when her time comes.

I wanted to mention some of the wildlife here in Arizona that we see. We see coyotes and javelina quite often. Sometimes we see the parents with the babies. At night, at work, we see them as they are out hunting and foraging for food. Sometimes at work, you can hear the coyotes howl all around you out in the desert. You know they are close.

We see lots of birds. The cutest are the quail with the baby quail. The parents are very protective of the babies. When they get ready to cross a road, one parent leads them while the other waits until the last baby is across and then he crosses too. The quail mostly run unless they have to fly. The babies are so cute and fast. We put water and birdseed out in the backyard and attract all kinds of birds. We get a lot of families of quail, and we get doves and cactus wrens. We see a roadrunner sometimes and the usual sparrows and wrens. We also have a finch feeder, so we get lots of very tiny birds on that.

The roadrunners are exciting to see. They are so distinctive and perky. They live on bugs, lizards, small snakes, and small birds. I saw one catch a small snake one time and watched it toss it around and fling it back and forth on the ground to kill it.

The doves are very docile and relaxed and nothing seems to bother them, except the quail chase them away from the food all of the time. The cactus wrens are very quick and perky and funny to watch. They are always on the move. We had a cactus wren build a nest in some cactus plants right near our gate at work. We also see nests of doves at work.

We see big and little owls at work. Some of the owls we see at night are huge. They are looking for rabbits and mice. The tiny owls perch on the fence posts and watch for supper to run by, which is usually a mouse or a small rabbit.

Out here in the desert are all kinds of creepy crawly things that crawl around, especially at night.

Since we work nights, we see lots of that kind of wildlife.

We see quite a few different kinds of snakes. Of course, you always are on the watch for rattlesnakes. You stay on the watch whether at work or at home at night. I have seen a lot of them at work over the years now.

Then there are the tarantulas. Yes, they are out here and come out mainly at night, so it behooves a person to watch where you are going at all times. Sometimes you even find them in the buildings. Needless to say, I hate this creature. Once I was in a building going down this long flight of stairs and I stepped to the next step and almost stepped on a huge one. It jumped, and I practically fell down the stairs trying to recover and get away. I have seen a lot of them outside and so am very careful at work. I use my flashlight quite a bit watching for them and for the rattlesnakes.

We also have to watch out for scorpions. They can grow very, very big out here. They can hurt if they sting you, and I guess they can even kill at times, so we are told.

Of course, there are all kinds of other spiders and bugs out at night. They are all over the place. If I ever get done working security at night, I will never set foot out of the house again after dark. Everything is a learning experience, and I have learned a lot here.

FAMILY TIES

I want to address the issue of family and how much that can help carry a person through life.

Mother and Daddy were excellent examples of love and selfless giving. Their entire lives were geared toward raising their four children and giving them the best that they could provide. This meant in every way. They were never money rich, but even in that respect, they did without so much so that we could have a chance at a good life.

They gave each one of us pride in ourselves and confidence to be able to meet life's problems. They raised us in the church and gave us a sound religious base upon which to build our own lives. As you can see in this record, Mother and Daddy gave us everything they could.

Mother and Daddy had a rich social outlet—again, based in family. Daddy had ten brothers and sisters in his family. As we were growing up, we had time to visit back and forth with our aunts and uncles and cousins. This extended family also fostered a sense of well-being and belonging for us. We had family reunions every so often, and the family, even today, feels the importance of continuing to carry on this tradition. All but one male of Daddy's immediate siblings have passed on now, but the legacy they left behind in their spouses, children, and grand- and great-grand children is never ending.

Mother only had one brother and a few cousins, but they also contributed to our leading a fuller life.

Mother and Daddy had another social outlet that was very important to them over all the years they lived. They both belonged to the Eastern Star. Daddy also belonged to the Masons. These were good organizations that my parents strongly believed in.

I wish to say a few words about my siblings, John, June, and Robert. They were always people I looked up to, even Robert, though he was younger. I looked up to him as he grew in his life.

All three of them nurtured their faith in the Lord and raised their families to do this too. So see what Mother and Daddy started? Numerous people for many generations came to know the Lord or will as time goes by.

John, my brother four years older, spent his life working in the computer field. John has three children and also grandchildren. He and his wife (Linda) have spent the last number of years as missionaries. They were first in the inner city of Philadelphia, PA. Later they were in the inner city of Oakland, CA. Now they have both retired and are spending some time traveling. They have been a blessing to me as they opened their home to me whenever I needed it. When we were both living in California and I was single, I always felt loved and wanted as they gave me a key to their home and said it was open to me anytime I wanted or needed it. They are both wonderful people.

My sister June is two years older than I. She and her husband (Phil) have two sons and also grandchildren from each of them. June also became a registered nurse and practiced only a short time at the beginning of her marriage. Then she stopped to raise her family. Later on she returned to school and got a master's degree in social work and has been working in that area since then. She has been a true friend and support to me all of my life.

Phil has spent his career teaching college chemistry and chairing the chemistry department at St. Mary's College in Notre Dame, Indiana. This is an oversimplification of his career by far. He was also right there when Mother needed someone to handle her financial affairs as she got on in years. He did a great job.

Robert, my younger brother by four years, and his wife (Vera) raised a fine family of four children. We lived close to them for many years and were able to watch their family grow and be nurtured. Robert spent his life in the Air force. He obtained his master's degree through the Air force. He is now out of the military but working as a contractor for the military. Vera did a lot of home schooling for each of their children and must have done a superb job, as they have all done well in college and school. They are all doing well in their lives.

My present family consists of Tom and Jennie and Michael. I also consider Jamie to be a part of my family, even though I have not seen him in a long time.

Tom and I have gotten along very well together

for most of our married lives. We have tried to sustain our faith and lives in the church.

Tom has a Bachelor of Arts Degree in Public Administration, which he obtained after he was out of the Navy and on his own. He is very intelligent and as I have indicated, has computer expertise that was self taught. Tom has a great sense of humor. We enjoy being with each other and cherish our time together. Tom loves my family and gets along great with all of them. Tom is my choice of partner, for the rest of either his or my life. We hope we can finish the work years and still have our health in order to enjoy some quality time with each other.

As you have been able to see, my own life has had many ups and downs. I have not always done the right or honorable thing. I have for many years wanted to seek the forgiveness of one old girlfriend, from years ago, but have never had the courage to do so. I only have the knowledge that I have received forgiveness through my Lord for that and for all my past mistakes. That is a great comfort. I know that when I die I will be in Heaven with the rest of my family.

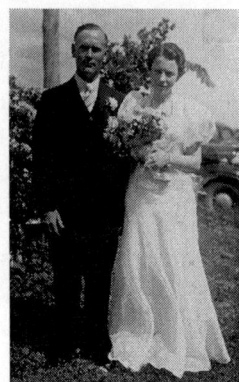

Mother and Daddy's wedding picture in 1938.

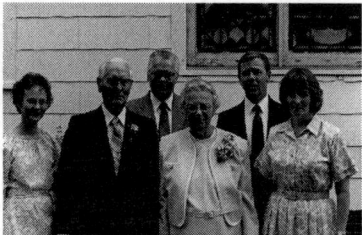

June, Dad, John, Mother, Robert, and myself for my parents 50th wedding anniversary.

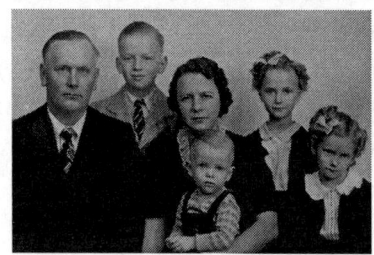

Our family portrait.

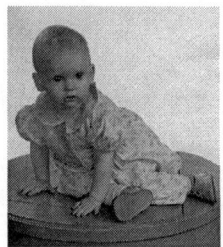

My baby picture in 1943.

ENDINGS

Maybe there are no endings. Maybe everything and everyone that disappears is actually beginning anew.

A few years ago, I went back to see the old farm I loved so much. It wasn't really there. The half-mile lane went in only about half that distance. It was weed covered. The house and all the buildings were gone. Even my beloved pig lot was gone. Everything had been turned into a perpetual field of crops that rotated every year. No young child would ever be able to look on it again as I did or love it as I had.

I think of all the pets that I have had during my lifetime that are now gone, like Corky who was with me through very hard times. Maybe that was her purpose and maybe it was not an ending when she died, but a beginning of new life to come. She was there so that my family now, Tom and Jennie and Michael, even knew her.

I think of the death of my father and mother. Though their deaths left me with lots of grief, maybe they had given me all that they could and their deaths were not an ending but a beginning. A new part of my life was starting to carry on their teachings and to become a better person for their having been here.

The best ending that they gave me was a belief in Jesus from the time I was a small child. This belief carried on throughout my life. The fact that this belief gives me eternal life is the best gift that a person can receive.

When I was in attendance during the time Mother was dying, I saw great evidence of her faith. I saw her renew her belief in the Lord and was reassured that she would be in Heaven when I arrived.

I have this comfort that all of my family and Tom will be in Heaven with me. There is no greater comfort than living life, knowing that the ending of it is really only a beginning—a beginning in eternity with my whole family and my Lord and Savior.

I have written this book because I saw all the stories that were going to be lost when my mother died. Several people have told me in the past that I should write a book, so this is my attempt. I want people to remember me when I am gone. I want our family to be remembered. Also, if nothing else, maybe this will lead someone else to the Lord.

I am 61 years old at the time of this writing. My birthday is 09–08–1943.

Contact Donna Merriam
www.donnamerriam.com
or order more copies of this book at

TATE PUBLISHING, LLC

127 East Trade Center Terrace
Mustang, Oklahoma 73064

(888) 361 - 9473

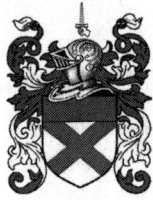

Tate Publishing, LLC

www.tatepublishing.com